The Will to Live

to Live

A Systematic Guide to our Reasons for Living

(Improved 2017)

Alistair J. Sinclair Ph.D.

Almostic Publications
2014

Published by

Almostic Publications

Glasgow

ISBN 978-0-9574044-2-7

© 2014, 2017 Alistair J. Sinclair

The right of Alistair J. Sinclair to be identified as the author of this book has been asserted by him in accordance with sections 77 & 78 of the Copyright and Patents Act of 1988

Other Works by
Alistair J. Sinclair

BOOKS

The Answers Lie Within Us
What is Philosophy: An Introduction
American Papers in Humanism and Religion
Sautonic Wisdom: What We Are Here To Do
The Promise of Dualism: An Introduction to Dualist Theory
Hale and Hearty: Looking at Things as a Whole
Advancing Humanity: The Need to Make Our Own Future
Belief Beyond Belief: Looking to the Better Future

E-BOOKS

The Future of Humanity: The Need to Believe in Humanity and its Future
Vindication: Justifying Our Existence
From Time to Eternity: An Essay on the Meaning of Time
Shakespeare on Time
Punish the Person not the Crime: A New Theory of Punishment Based on
Old Principles
Old Age, Death and the After-Life
Reforming the British Constitution
The Normal Society: And How To Get It

Contents

Preface

The usefulness of living lies not in duration but in what you make of it. Some have lived long and lived little. See to it while you are still here. Whether you have lived enough depends not on a count of years but on your will.

Michel de Montaigne, *The Complete Essays*, trans. M.A. Screech, London: Penguin, 1991, Essay XX, p.106

Forward and frolic glee was there,
The will to do, the soul to dare.

Sir Walter Scott, *The Lady of the Lake,* Canto First, XXI, 413-4

The will to live makes life worth living. It keeps us going when the going gets tough. It is the inner strength we summon up when we really need it. It acts as a unifying power within us that helps us to continue living in spite of all difficulties we face. Our strength of purpose depends on our inner will keeping us together. We don't need artificial stimulants to keep us going if the will to live is sufficiently strong. All those film stars, rock stars and celebrities, who have died young through overdoses or over-indulgence of some kind, seem to have lacked sufficient will to keep going. They needed drugs, drink, bizarre sex or whatever as they couldn't face life without thrills and spills. They couldn't live quietly with themselves from day-to-day as there was not enough in them to make them at ease with themselves. They lived for the moment and their moods got the better of them as they had no control over their feelings. It is argued here, that if the will to live is sufficiently strong and well-developed, we need no more than our own inner resources to make life worthwhile.

Those who lack the will to live may even contemplate suicide, if not commit it. They may even regard their lives as so worthless that they kill other people whose lives they regard as equally worthless. Mass killers have given up on life entirely; therefore they wish to deprive as many people as possible of the privilege of living. To combat such negativity, we need reasons for living that enhance the value of our lives. The more reasons we have, the stronger our will to live for the best possible purposes. The active search for reasons for living helps us to develop the will within us, and there is much we can do to aid its development.

Our sustained enjoyment of life is based in our will or inner being. When we cease enjoying the simple, everyday things in life such as going to work, watching television, participating in sport, computer games and so on, life can lose its lustre. We can only look within ourselves and find

v

more and better reasons for living. By opening our minds to the opportunities before us, we can think our way out of such existential emptiness. One way of doing this is to consult the range of possibilities available to us, and the content of this book may be helpful in that regard.

This book offers a systematic guide to the principal reasons why we live and why we are here. It contains a wide range of possible answers to the question 'What are we here for?' These answers are arranged in a systematic way and are analysed systematically. We all face the problem of living and of making the most of our lives. The more answers we consider, the more we can see the possibilities of life and living. Thus, the aim is to bolster the will to live and build up the inner strength needed to combat the self-deprecatory and suicidal responses to life to which we are all prone if we allow ourselves to get into a negative frame of mind.

The primary list of thirty-six reasons explicated in this book is not exhaustive. The list is supplemented in the text by 'Ancillary Answers' which are added to each of these primary reasons. There are doubtless many more reasons for living not covered here but usually they are associated with one or other of these primary reasons. For example, football fanatics may behave as if their answer is 'We are here to play football or support a football team'. But this response can be considered ancillary to 'We are here to enjoy ourselves' or 'We are here to please ourselves'. It belongs to the same category of responses that are relatively limited and selfish approaches to life. The complete list of reasons can be seen below.

This guide is unique at least in the way it is categorised and ordered, and also in the way in which they are explicated. It is hopefully a useful contribution to self-help literature. It originated as a list of reasons for living compiled for a 'What Are We Here For?' class held at the University of Strathclyde, Glasgow during 2003-04. It has since been developed as a systematic guide in the manner outlined below.

Introduction

What this book is about

No one really knows why we are here. Anyone who pretends to know with any certainty is invariably a bigot, charlatan, demagogue, would-be prophet or whatever. Any answers are a matter of belief not knowledge or truth. But we need not give up the quest before we even start. Our ignorance of such matters hasn't stopped people in the past from finding reasons for living, nor should it do so now or at any time in the future. The history of humankind is based on the reasons concocted by successive cultures. Each culture has found reasons of its own to contribute something of value and interest to civilisation. The diversity of world culture is the better for these differing contributions. However, the flaws and deficiencies inherent in these reasons for living have often contributed to the eventual downfall of these cultures. But they would have achieved nothing without them, just as we produce nothing of value as individuals unless we have reasons of our own that are worth living for.

This book explores the most obvious and fundamental reasons for living that may have occurred to anyone at one time or another. It is a guide that invites readers to choose for themselves which answers are best or most appropriate for them. Its purpose is to show the ranges of choices available and to stimulate thought about them. These choices consist in a wide range of answers to the question, 'What are we here for?' These answers take the form of 'reasons for living'. We are here for a reason because we are capable of finding reasons for living when we make the effort to find them. In looking to ourselves for reasons for living, we can find answers that make sense of what we are doing with our lives. The stock phrase, 'We are here to . . .', indicates both an answer to the question, 'What are we here for?' and a reason why we are living and what we are living for.

The result is not an exhaustive list of all reasons whatsoever as the book is only a brief guide to the subject and not a complete or all-encompassing study of the whole field. There are doubtless as many answers to the question, 'Why are we here?' as there are human beings to formulate them and forms of human activity which constitute answers to the question. But the thirty-six answers mentioned below have been selected for the purposes of this book. The main reasons for selecting them are outlined in each chapter concerning them. As can be seen below, these thirty-six answers have been arranged in twelve triads according to how they relate to similar answers.

A personal view is given here of our most commonly acknowledged reasons for living and an even more personal account of what these reasons mean. No single individual has a monopoly of understanding all there is to know. We all owe it to ourselves to find our own answers since relying on other people's answers may diminish our uniqueness and deprive civilisation of our contribution to it. No doubt many repetitions, inconsistencies, incoherencies, and incompatibilities will be found among the statements constituting this book. No apology is offered for this as the whole purpose of the book is to get people thinking about these things for themselves.

What this book aims to do

The main aim is not to bombard readers with a vain litany of facts but to encourage them to become wiser and more insightful by thinking their way through the options listed in this book. Readers should not work their way through this book as if it were a novel. They should dip serendipitously into this *pot-pourri* of choices. In this way, they may increase their self-understanding by stimulating their powers of judgment and evaluation. This emphasises the value of wisdom by showing how they can use their judgment to make worthwhile choices between courses of action based on what they expect to gain from making these choices. The integrity of self is thereby enhanced by relating all these choices to one's principal purposes in life.

Getting oneself together by grasping oneself as a whole is a step towards achieving wisdom. Being wise consists in doing one's best for the best possible reasons. But knowing what is best means taking the largest possible view of things at the time that one makes a decision. One takes into account the greatest possible range of factors that one is capable of comprehending at any moment in time. It is only possible to do this effectively when one is touch with oneself and all one's past experiences and skills so that one marshals oneself appropriately to meet the demands of the occasion and to cope with them effectively.

This book is not meant to make life easy. Whatever choices we make in life, problems will arise from them. However, the book may help to ease the problem of choosing how to live. It is a guide to many of the most obvious reasons for living though by no means all of them. The range of human interests and activities is such that there may be an infinite number of reasons of living, or at least as many as there are human beings to think of them.

To make the most of our lives, we need as many reasons for living that we can think of.   They can help us to strengthen our resolve to live as well and as fully as we are physically capable of doing. We may have reasons for living which we are not fully aware of or which we don't put into words. We may even deny that we have any reasons for living but that usually means that we can't think of them or bring them to mind or that we find our present ones to be inadequate or unconvincing.

These choices are not meant to be rigorously compatible with each other. The fact that they are mentioned here does not mean that I personally condone or approve of them as choices. It is merely pointed out that people have made such choices in the past and no doubt will do so in the future. They think that they have valid or worthwhile reasons for making such choices, or they may have no reasons at all, and do so for a whim, a laugh or whatever.

The reasons for living discussed in this book are not enforced on anyone. They are hypothetical rather than categorical imperatives. They offer choices that are contingent upon one's feelings, circumstances, health and other purely personal matters. Categorical imperatives may concern our responsibilities to other people, to society and to ourselves. They may be necessary for our health and happiness, as in the case of medical knowledge. However, the reasons for living in this book may contribute to health and happiness but they cannot guarantee them. Therefore they are not to be regarded as sacrosanct or inviolable principles. They are suggestions contingent upon the needs and interests of the individual and not on what is necessary for them to know or to do.

It is important that none of the answers discussed in this book are treated as ends in themselves. They are all means to other ends that are beyond any single of them. The ultimate ends are those encompassing many answers. These ends are ultimately ethical since they concern the best we can do to benefit life and humanity. By consulting as many answers as possible we are better able to think of our life as a whole, and how posterity will be view our deeds and the value of our lives.

No one has all the answers but that fact need not stop anyone from looking for possible answers to these questions. Being able to look for answers means that we will do so, for as long as our curiosity and spirit of intellectual adventure leads us on, regardless of the consequences. Our curiosity and open-mindedness have served us well so far, and there is no reason for them to cease. However, our adventuring must always have an ethical basis. 'Can' depends not on 'if' but on 'should', or 'ought', 'should not' or 'ought not', since our ability to do anything should or ought to be governed or limited by ethical or judgmental factors. We can't just do anything because we can do it but because of the good outcomes that may ensue. The possible beneficial outcomes are our best reasons for doing things. Thus, in looking for the best answers concerning what to do with our lives we find good reasons for living. These reasons help us not only to continue to live but also to do something positive and worthwhile with our lives. This implies that we are here to move on. We are not meant be totally static, catatonic, vegetative entities, like Buddhist or yogic meditators. This is the difference between being an animal and being a vegetable; the animation of the one and the vegetativeness of the other.

Therefore, the main aim of this guide is bolster our will to live by providing reasons for living that combat negative responses more concerned with dying than with living. Extreme examples of these negative responses include the following:

Self-Defeating Responses

➢ *The Mortal Answer:*   We are here to die.
➢ *The Homocidal Answer:* We are here to kill each other.
➢ *The Suicidal Answer:*   We are here to kill ourselves.

These answers are self-defeating because they betray an obsession with death, dying, and particularly with one's own death. The continuity of the self depends on the continuance of life. It defeats the purposes of life to be obsessed with death and killing. Any event that brings an end to life threatens not only the self but also its integrity, as the vitality of the self concerns the business of living and not dying.   In other words, our personality is developed through living one's life and is retarded by a pre-occupation on death and the termination of life. The will to continue living is diminished if, from one moment to the next, all that one is thinking about is death or dying.

Killing another person is self-defeating in that one is killing something of oneself in so doing. We naturally identify with other people when we sympathise with them and their feelings. Thus, we kill a part of ourselves by killing another person in so far as we can identify with that person. Even if we have no feelings at all about a victim, the act of murder destroys the humanity within us and we lessen ourselves thereby. The psychopathic sociopath has no excuses for their behaviour since they can't deny being a human being. Contempt for humanity means also being contemptuous of ourselves since we are a part of humanity whether we like it or not.

It is easy to say that there is more to life than simply dying. But saying so does nothing to alleviate the state of mind in which a person is obsessed with death, dying and killing. We are all capable of entering into a frame of mind in which life seems so vapid and meaningless that only death seems to make sense of it. One simply gives up on life when such answers dominate one's thinking. In short, these answers are not only self-defeating but reflect a pathological state of mind which is contrary to a healthy, normal outlook on life. We really need to focus on the positive reasons for living if we are to avoid such negativity. This book therefore concentrates mainly on the optimistic view of why we are here and what we are to do with ourselves. Negativity is no more than a needless attitude of mind.

Do we really need reasons for living?

It is perfectly possible to live without having any reasons for living. Other animals don't need such reasons since they live largely in response to present exigencies. They don't see their lives as a whole; therefore they don't worry too much about the future. In contrast, we humans are always striving to make more of our lives. Especially when we are young, we can become obsessed with our future and with finding ways to better it. Thus, we are typically dissatisfied with our lot and want to improve it. Some people seem to live contented lives without wanting more than they already have. Their reasons for living seem to be minimal. If they can get along without them, then that's fine. But scratch the surface and you will almost certainly find discontent lurking beneath. When they think about it, they can find reasons for living differently from they are at present. This is simply because we are rationalising beings. We are capable of finding reasons for whatever we do, however bizarre, abnormal or unnatural that activity may appear to other people. Whoever poses the question to themselves, 'What am I here for?' must be capable of providing some kind of answer to it, whether or not these answers satisfy them or not. 'I am here to sit and watch television everyday', 'I am here to eat, drink and have a laugh', are examples of the most trivial answers that anyone can give when they pose that question to themselves. This raises the question of whether such answers are good enough even for the person providing them. Even they may admit that there ought to be more to life than living for such trivial reasons.

Everything that we do betrays what we are and represents our mode of living. Thus, every time we rationalise what we are doing, we find reasons for our living in the way that we do. These need not be reasons for living, but in practice we are concocting them all the time because we are continually making sense of our lives for our own benefit, and continually justifying our actions to other people.

Those who go further and say that there never can be any reasons why we are here, have overlooked their own reasons for living. They must have some reasons for living otherwise they would not trouble themselves to get out of bed, feed themselves or do or say anything whatsoever. What would be the point? If they are doing anything at all with their lives, then they must be doing it for a reason, such as to feel better, get drunk, or have a laugh. The latter reasons are reasons for living whether they are acknowledged as such or not. No one does anything for no reason at all and anything that they do for a reason explains why they are continuing to live. We can all find reasons for whatever we are doing with our lives and these reasons give us a rationale for making something out of our lives rather than nothing. What this book offers is a comprehensive list of the most important and obvious of these reasons for living.

What reasons for living are needed for

Reasons for living are needed to make sense of our lives. By doing so, we can come to terms with the limited nature of life, and with the fact that we can do only so much with our lives as we have only a limited period of time within which to live them. If we take our lives seriously then we have the problem of filling them so that they are not absurd, meaningless or filled with nonsense. The reasons for living provide a rationale for living one's life no matter what the obstacles and difficulties which life throws in our way. In times of crisis or uncertainty, we may need reasons for continuing to live from day to day. We need to reinforce our belief in these reasons from time to time and, if necessary, rethink them to convince ourselves of their validity and applicability.

Just asking the question 'what are we here for?' usually means that we are looking for reasons about why we are here and what we are supposed to do with our lives. If I ask myself what I am here for, I can tell myself that I am here to do certain things with my life. I can list these things and show how the ways in which I am or am not living my life in conformity with these things. These might be called reasons why I value my life and continue to live in spite of all the ups and downs, trials and tribulations which life throws in our faces. This guide hopefully suggests ways in which this listing can be done.

If I do not value my life then I must consider myself a worthless person. If my life means nothing to me then I mean nothing to myself. And I have no reason to value the lives of others since they are no better than I am. As our whole culture depends on the self-respect and self-esteem of its participants, it is threatened when they lack all reasons for valuing themselves or others. Thus, the future of our society depends on everyone continuing to have self-worth and to do meaningful things with their lives.

We are after all less than human in so far as we fail to find a rational place in society. Having such a place makes our lives more meaningful in specific ways because we are given more reasons to be proud of ourselves as useful people. Thus, unemployed people typically feel their lives to be empty and aimless because they lack the ties and security of regular employment to make their lives more fulfilled. The purpose of society is to give everyone without exception the opportunities of life consonant with their abilities and aspirations. As society becomes better organised and increasingly complex, the greater are opportunities on offer. Thus, it is in all our interests to contribute as best we can to the increased development and improved organisation of society. This is ultimately the purpose of human society to which we should all subscribe.

Our difficulty in finding answers for ourselves

Being human means potentially having an existential angst (or anxiety) concerning the meaning of life. Nearly all of us at one time or another have wondered about life in general and our role in it. Our bewilderment may be reflected in questions such as: 'What is life all about?', 'Why am I here?', 'Why am I living at all?', and 'What is the point of it all?' But the tendency is for us to look for one answer to these questions which will resolve our anxiety and uncertainty once and for all. Having found that one answer we cease our questioning and rest on our laurels. But it is a mistake to assume that there is one simple and straightforward answer to all these questions. The one answer which we settle for at one time, may turn out to be illusory in the long run. It is better to admit that there is no ultimate 'Holy Grail' but only a never-ending quest (in the original Arthurian tales, the Grail appeared to the knights only in dreams or collective visions). The only valid answer lies in the activity of looking for answers which are constantly sought without lasting success. Life is a quest to perfect and complete such answers without arriving at any conclusion, bar death itself.

Clearly, the question 'What are we here for?' admits of no simple answer. Indeed, this book can only be a guide suggesting how to look for answers to that question. No single answer to the question 'what are we here for?' can be the final one since we are constantly moving on during our lives and often find other answers more relevant to our changing aims and aspirations. Thus, the meta-answer that goes beyond all the answers in this book is not workable answer but more of an explanation and a challenge: 'We are here to explain why we are here and to look for these answers for ourselves'. In finding our own reasons why we are here, we are explaining our own existence, and finding our own rationale for continuing to be. To that extent, we are self-reflective beings constantly turning in on ourselves to try and get to the bottom of what we are. This basic problem of living must be solved by everyone and by every generation and it admits of no final or easy solution.

Our difficulty in answering the question: 'What are we here for?' is common to us all, and answering it involves us all. By universalising that question, we can arrive at answers that are relevant to us as individuals. We universalise it by seeing it from other people's point of view. What is good enough for other people is often good enough for us. It is a question of what we want to settle for as individuals. In thinking these things out for ourselves, we are also thinking universally because we use the word, phrases, sentences and general conceptions which are universal currency. We cannot escape the prison of language that dictates to us what we can or cannot think about. Thus, language in the end makes social beings out of us since we can only rationalise our lives in terms that others can make sense of.

Moreover, any answers to such questions only invite further questions *ad infinitum*. They offer yet more puzzles and paradoxes to be unravelled and thought about. The wide variety of reasons for our living provided here are not meant to be sacrosanct or inviolable. The aim is to invite controversy rather than eliminate it as in the authoritarian belief systems. This approach thrives on controversy since it recognises the disputatious nature of all matters relating to what we are or are not to do with our lives. There is always the prospect that in the future a better and more comprehensive account may be possible as the facts of the universe make themselves more manifest to us.

The scientific compatibility of reasons for living

An attempt is made in this book to give as full an account as possible of what we are here for, given the present facts of science. The 'we' usually referred to here is specifically the human race. No attempt is made to give an account that is valid for all time. This account is only relevant to the present day and to the present state of our knowledge. As mere human beings, we are not in possession of all the facts of the universe or of all the reasons why we are here and what life is really all about. Therefore, no account can possibly be the last word on such matters and this account is only an attempt to improve on all previous ones, which have been mainly religious, superstitious, dogmatic and often insulting to our intelligence.

Each increase in our understanding of the universe adds meaning to our lives because an item is being added to our corpus of knowledge which did not exist previously. The fact that the universe is something rather than nothing means that we ourselves are something rather than nothing because we are a product of that development and an inextricable part of the universe. Our relationship to the universe may be ultimately unfathomable and it may be that the physical sciences have only begun to unravel its depth and complexity. Quantum mechanics already shows that there are mysteries at the heart of the universe. The extent to which we are intimately connected to the universe as a whole is becoming more apparent. Our increasing knowledge in this sphere contributes our individual quests for self-understanding as it is important to arrive at a coherent view of our place in the universe, however provisional that may be.

In that regard, the various reasons for living constitute a link between the individual and the universe. When we look at our lives as a whole, we are universalising them and seeing them from afar. Thus, the ultimate answer to the meaning of life is one that links us to the universe as a whole. From that perspective we can see the true value of our lives. This perspective is the true one because we are products of the universe. We all owe our lives to the holistic outcome of the universe in its development towards creating entities of ever-increasing complexity. Originally, we were all no more than stardust. But this tells us nothing about what we are as human beings. There is nothing in the stardust that could have predicted what we are now. It is more interesting to consider how much more than just stardust we are now. For example, we now know more about the universe than the universe itself can know about itself. Due to our scientific knowledge our relationship to the universe and to life on Earth is now hugely complicated in its detail. Even more interesting is what we are meant to do about this existence of ours which the natural processes of the universe have made possible. This is what we all have to find out for ourselves and hopefully this book helps the individual to do so.

Thus, in summary, all the answers we arrive at in seeking reasons for living reflect the way we have emerged and developed as a species in the universe and on this planet. From an idealistic point of view, each of these answers tends towards all the others when they are unified in terms of what the universe means to us both as a species and as individuals. Paradoxically, by referring them to the universe as a whole and by expanding their meaning by such a reference, we bring them down-to-earth and show how they enter into our everyday lives. This is achieved by self-reference: by referring these abstractions to our own lives in terms of our emergence from the universe and our inevitable submergence into the dust of the universe. Everything within these two events constitutes what we are as human beings. Thus, the attempt to apply all these answers to our own lives puts us idealistically in touch with the universe as a whole.

The value of this approach

The range of human potentialities explored in this book is very comprehensive. It tells no one which of the given answers to choose or how to live. It is advisory rather than authoritative as it presents options and allows people to make of them what they will. An honest account of the merits and demerits of each answer is attempted. It is for the reader to make final judgments about the appropriateness of these answers from their point of view. This approach hopefully reinforces their ability to welcome opposing views which negate and criticise the arguments developed within the corpus of this work. This is deliberate because only by continuous dialogue with opposing views can the body of knowledge be refined, corrected, made more up-to-date, relevant to contemporary conditions and so on.

Instead of relying on the blind faith or dogmatic belief which religion offers, this book advocates that we should actively find for ourselves reasons to justify our living at all. The activity of continually seeking and vindicating such reasons gives us the best foundation for self-belief. The reasons for living given here are not themselves the foundation. In being apprehended by each individual for themselves, these reasons become self-made and subjectively based, and they are correspondingly provisional and indefinite. What is solid, enduring and perennial is the constant activity of looking for them and refining them. This makes this unending quest personal to each of us and not just something concerning the abstracted interests of humanity in general.

Because our reasoning powers are limited and fallible, many say that we have no business thinking about such unfathomable matters. They maintain that these matters are to be left to God, whatever that is taken to mean. But this is an abrogation of our responsibility to ourselves to use our own reasoning powers such as they are. We are justified in doing so as long as it is done in the full knowledge of the fallible and provisional nature of the knowledge gleaned from them. However, the extent to which our reasoning powers may be relied upon for these purposes is not dealt with in this book as it is the subject of my work on the subject of contextual logic which is the holistic counterpart of deductive logic.

The hope is that this book obviates the need for religion in so far as religion tells us what we are here for. It is obvious that this book offers a much richer range of answers to that question than any religion can. It does not replace religion in respect of the mysticism and unfathomability of religious experience. But it surely gives a more realistic and comprehensive view of the possibilities and choices of life that are open to us.

We live in a culture that is torn between the old religious view of majestic man made in the image of God and the new scientific view of human beings as being the random product of evolutionary events over which we have no control. The former view is largely discredited by the power of the scientific view but the latter cannot supersede the religious view while it demeans human beings by reducing us to mere amalgams of atoms and molecules lost in a limitless universe. Equally, the religious view demeans us in comparison with an indefinable God whose existence is a perennial puzzle. The happy medium between these extreme views must be worked out and my writings constitute a preliminary attempt to do so. We need reasons for building ourselves up and for making more of ourselves and not less, as both the scientific and religious views tend to do. These reasons need to be better than those offered by both these views, whether or not there is evidence to support these reasons.

Using this guide to create a life plan

Nobody knows how to live the perfect life but we can always to do our best to make life better than it is at any point in time. A life plan can help us to focus our activities in definite directions depending on the choices we make. It challenges us to take a realistic view of our lives and what we can do with them. It identifies the respects in which life can be improved and enriched. It is not concerned with improving the physical side of life. There are gyms, health centres and plenty of other organisations which can improve physical health and well-being. A life plan looks to intellectual, mental, social, and cultural improvement. Above all, it should result in a better person more fit for human society than hitherto.

A life plan deals with what we want to do with our life and how we want to go about it. We begin by assessing what life is about and where it is or is not going. We look at the reasons of living with that assessment in mind and we organise our chosen reasons for living into a coherent plan of action. We make a plan of what we want to do with life by looking at each of the alternative choices mentioned in this book. We put together as many as possible of the choices which seem reasonable and attractive to we. A certain amount of 'pick and mix' choice is involved here. We then have to consider the extent to which these choices might conflict with each other and eliminating conflicting choices as far as possible. The life plan results from the systematic connections that we make between these choices to make a consistent plan of life. A system of thought is thereby constructed in which a pattern of life choices is established. All our reasons for living are put together in relation to each other and to what our ends and goals in life are. These reasons for living are thereby chosen in a definite pattern which comes together in a coherent life plan.

We need the courage of our convictions in making our choices. The greater the quantity and the broader the choices that we make then the more proof we have against the flaws and deficiencies which are inherent all reasons for living. Reasons for living can then be a bulwark against the inadequacies of our reasoning powers and the vagaries of fortune.

The Structure and Use of This Guide

Thirty-six answers to the question 'What are we here for?' are discussed in detail in this book. They are divided up into twelve triads or groups of three. These divisions are perhaps more pleasingly symmetrical than they are logical or scientific. But there is serious thinking behind them and the reasons for making each division are given at the beginning of each chapter under the heading 'What's elementary, universal etc. . . .about them?' These reasons are of course open to question, as are all reasons whatsoever. Each of these thirty-six responses comprises a **main** answer to which **ancillary** answers are added where and when appropriate. Each answer is discussed under a standard set of headings. These are as follows:

'What this answer means'
'What this answer is good for'
'What's wrong with it'
'Treating it as one thing'
'Treating it as one of many'
'Putting it into practice'
'Ancillary answers'

These standard headings are also supplemented occasionally by additional headings which vary according to the nature of the answer under discussion. Finally, each chapter ends with a comparison and assessment of the three answers under the heading of 'What can we make of these answers?'

'What this answer means'

Each answer is analysed and elaborated in terms of its meaning and implications. The problem is of course that every answer can mean something different to every individual who makes it a feature of their lives. Thus, anything said here is can only be a guide or indication of what the answer is often interpreted as meaning. The object is to stimulate thinking on the matter and not to settle the matter for all time. It is virtually impossible to settle matters in that way because every statement and every elaboration itself raises questions and create puzzles in people's minds. So far from sorting things out, the more that is said on such matters the greater the possibilities for misunderstanding and confusion. More perplexity and bewilderment is the likely result. This is good in so far as it gets people thinking rather than resting on past presuppositions which may be quite wrong. But it is also bad in that there is no end to this postponement of action, just as mere talking engenders yet more talk instead of reaching a decisive conclusion. Ultimately, the exigencies of any situation terminate thought and talk and make action necessary.

'What this answer is good for'

This assesses the usefulness and applicability of the answer. In so far as an answer is good for something then it must have helpful or useful consequences in being put into practice. It is good in the sense suggesting or fostering worthwhile action or appropriate behaviour. There is obviously an ethical dimension here or at the very least an evaluation of some sort. What it is ultimately good for has to be decided by everyone for themselves. The given account is only one point of view concerning what these answers are good for.

'What's wrong with it'

To ask what is wrong with any particular answer is to question its range and applicability. It doesn't matter how sensible, logical, obvious, attractive, or commonsensical the reason for living may appear to be; it is still a fallible and human reason and therefore subject to faults and deficiencies which can be criticised and objected to. Thus, it is desirable to be clear about these faults and deficiencies even though one believes most fervently in the efficacy of the answer being examined. Indeed, the more fanatical a person's belief in any one answer, the more it is necessary that the faults and limitations should be pointed out to that person.

'Treating it as one thing'

When the application of an answer becomes an end in itself then it is being treated as one thing. It becomes something aimed at for its own sake and regardless of the value or importance of other approaches. The account given under this heading is the monistic view of how the particular answer is treated. A monistic view treats the answer as being the one and only answer worthy of serious consideration, as compared with all the alternative answers that are offered in this book. This view is usually involves a dogmatic treatment of the answer. It is treated as if it were the one and only answer to the question 'What are we here for?' A person taking this view will live their lives round their favoured answer on which they cling as if it were a crutch. Everything in their lives is referred back to this answer. As a result they live a much narrower and circumscribed life than they would if they had not allowed themselves to be dominated and hamstrung by this one approach to the problem of living. Each of the answers becomes idealised beyond its practical importance when it is concentrated on to the exclusion of all the others. It becomes a dogmatic ideal which is not only unattainable in the long run but is also harmful even when it is attainable.

The English essayist William Hazlitt wrote a diverting essay called 'On People With One Idea' which begins, "There are people who have but one idea: at least, if they have more, they keep it a secret, for they never talk but of one subject." Hazlitt points out that such people will guide every conversation round to their favourite topic. Such people have found their answer which possesses them for the rest of their life, or until they get out of the dogmatic and lazy state of mind which prevents them seeing any other answer.

'Treating it as one among many'

This refers to the pluralistic view of what these answers. It is encapsulated in the saying: *e pluribus unum* - one out of many (which prior to 1956 was the motto of the USA). The pluralistic view follows from treating the answer as being one among many possible answers even though it may be considered to be more important or valuable than some or all of the others. The weaknesses of one answer may be mitigated by its links with other answers. Thus, the pluralistic view is implicitly assumed to be the correct approach to applying specific answer as a reason for living. Each answer may have harmful consequences when it is pursued single-mindedly and in disregard of the alternatives. They are less likely to have harmful consequences if they are part of a life plan that includes many answers to the problem of what to do with one's life. The account given under the heading of 'pluralistic treatment' is usually quite critical of the answer being discussed. Its limitations are pointed out because the value of other answers are being recognised as paying an equal, if not greater, part in our lives. The pluralistic treatment also admits the possibility of linking these answers to other answers as part of more comprehensive life plan as mentioned above.

'Putting it into practice'

The extent to which each answer can be put into practice is discussed and elaborated. This includes the pitfalls and difficulties which inevitably arise when any answer to the problem of life is applied to everyday life. None of these answers promises any straightforward solutions to the everyday problems of life. Putting them into practice means using them to plan one's life better, to make important decisions concerning one's future, to improve one's lifestyle, and so on.

'Ancillary answers'

The word 'ancillary' means subsidiary or supplementary and it is applied to those answers which are added on to the main answers being dealt with in depth. The ancillary answers are generally implied by or closely related to the answers to which they are linked in the text. They may even be considered by some people to be more appropriate for in-depth treatment than the ones they supplement. However, they are usually closely enough related to the main answers to be largely explained by the account given of the latter. For example, we can arrive at more personal answers such as 'I am here to do my best for my family and friends', and 'I am here to do my best for my colleagues'. These answers are ancillary to the Moral Answer which is: *'We are here to do our best and to make life better for ourselves and others'* as can be seen below. There are doubtless more ancillary answers than are mentioned in this book but this is only a brief guide to the subject and it is up to the reader to supply any perceived deficiencies as they so wish.

The List of the Reasons Discussed Here

Part One - The Contemplative Approach

Part Two - The Productive Approach

12. Self -Sacrificing Responses

➤ *The Self-Penalising Answer:* We are here to suffer and live in pain. 123
➤ *The Great Cause Answer:* We are here to sacrifice ourselves to a
cause greater than ourselves.   125
➤ *The Self-Immolating Answer:* We are here to sacrifice ourselves
for the sake of others.   128

In asking the question 'Why are we here?' and in arriving at answers such as those above, we begin giving ourselves reasons for continuing to live and for making something of our lives. If we can arrive at meaningful and worthwhile answers, our lives may acquire more purpose and a greater sense of direction than they would otherwise have. Our constantly seeking the answers in terms of our own lives is also expressive of our freewill. We are free to please ourselves concerning which answers interest us most at any point of time during our lives. The main thing is not to be dominated by just one answer throughout our lives since that is the essence of personal slavery and unfreedom.

The above answers to the question, 'Why are we here?' are among the most important ones because they are fundamental to the human condition. Unravelling their meaning helps us to understand better the human predicament and our place in the universe, as has been argued above. For not one of these answers is sufficient in itself to make us what we are as human beings. We need to bear in mind as many answers as possible to bring out our humanness in its entirety. In this way we learn to behave humanely, that is to say, with as much human affection and forbearance towards others as we are capable of achieving. All these answers are vital and important in themselves in making their particular contribution to the human condition. As individuals we tend to stress one or more of these but seldom if ever stress all of them all of the time.

Part One
The Contemplative Approach

1
Elementary Responses

➢   *The 'To Be' Answer:* **We are here to be or to exist.**
➢   *The 'To Do' Answer:* **We are here to do or to act.**
➢   *The 'To Have' Answer:* **We are here to have or to hold.**

What's Elementary About Them?

These answers are elementary in that they are the basis on which other answers may be built and they are not enough in themselves. The natural response to them is to ask, 'to be what?', 'to do what?', or 'to have what?' It is what we are here **for** that interests us and not the obvious fact that we are here. These are intransitive verbs which have no object and therefore no goal beyond the mere activity of being, doing, or having.

However, these answers are less elementary when they acquire a religious dimension and become ends towards religious goals such as aiming for purity or holiness, or fulfilling religious rituals or ceremonies. But they are still intransitive in that they have no real object beyond the vacuous religious activity or ritual. Such activities may simply pander to the feelings of the people engaged in them and have no meaning or significance outside of them. Rituals indeed are a type of play or game that at least keep people out of mischief.

The psychologist Erich Fromm wrote a book called *To Be or To Have?** in which he argued that western society is too much into having and not enough into being. But such a judgment is culturally relative. We may be living in a thoroughly materialistic society at the moment. However, the solution to the extremes of materialism is not to lurch to other extreme of spirituality. The solution is to explain both of these extremes by system of thought that goes beyond them. This has been the time honoured role of philosophy, as I argue in my book, *What is Philosophy* (Dunedin Academic Press, 2008).

* Erich Fromm, *To Be or To Have?* 1976 – London: Sphere Books, 1979.

These answers were satirised in a once popular piece of graffiti:

'To be is to do' - Aristotle

'To do is to be' - Sartre

'Do be, do be' - Sinatra

The last line refers to the refrain of Frank Sinatra's song 'Strangers in the Night'. Arguably, it sums up the vacuity of late twentieth century philosophy and its failure to deal with the big questions.

The 'To Be' Answer:
We are here to be or to exist

What this answer means:

On the face of it, this answer means very little since it tells us the obvious, namely, that we are or exist. Existence is not so much the problem as its content, or rather its potential content. Even the well-known passage from Hamlet 'To be or not be, that is the question' is now rendered into contemporary English as 'To live or not to live. That is the issue.'[*] This not only clarifies for the modern reader the association of Hamlet's words with suicide, it also implies that being is not enough. Continuing to live, one's reasons for wanting to live, and what one does with that life; these are the problems. Hamlet is questioning himself because he seeks reasons for continuing to live. Nowadays it is not enough simply to be or to exist, there needs also to be some point to the fact of living. This is an important shift of emphasis, perhaps brought about existentialist thinking which, especially in Sartre's version, stresses the importance of essence over mere existence. It is not enough to be; it is necessary to develop one's 'essence' or what there is within us to be developed. Hence this book is concerned with reasons for living rather than with reasons for being.

What this answer is good for:

This answer is good for pinpointing the importance of our existing at all. It draws attention to the obvious point that unless we exist we can't be or do anything. Without being or existence, we are good for nothing. Of course, we can feel ourselves to be good for nothing whatever we do in life. But even to feel that way is not nothing. It merely signifies the pain and uncertainty of living. We always yearn for more out of life than what we

---

[*] *Hamlet,* Act Three, Scene One. The modern rendering is from Shakespeare Made Easy - Hamlet, edited and rendered into modern English by Alan Durband, London: Hutchinson, 1986, p. 143.

actually get. No matter how much we get out of life, there is always the possibility of getting more. We often miss what we don't get, more than we appreciate what we do get out of life. To counter these feelings, we must count our blessings, always look on the bright side of life, and so on. For in the last analysis, it is a blessing to be alive at all.

Ever since Aristotle constructed his metaphysics (or more accurately his 'first philosophy') around the notion of being or existence, metaphysicians have made a great deal out of this, not least Hegel and the existentialists. The latter made even more out of the notion of 'nothing' with which being is to be contrasted. We are constantly combating nothingness in making our choices and in striving to fill our lives with meaning. In so far as we don't want to be nonentities for whom life is meaningless, we must struggle to make something of our lives.

What's wrong with it:

This answer is deficient not only in its lack of content. It is also deficient in meaning because it tells us nothing about what existence is about and what it is for. It is a tautologous answer that begs the question and merely attributes existence and beingness to things and events that are already known to exist or to be because they are there. Existence and beingness accompanies every thing and event which we perceive or conceive therefore we express nothing new by saying that they exist or be.

There is also a deficiency in treating the verbs 'to exist' and 'to be' as if they were synonyms. As this answer stands, it provides no way of telling whether or not the verbs 'to be' and 'to exist' are being treated as synonyms or whether they are being distinguished from each other in some unspecified way. Usually the verb 'to exist' is used to emphasise the fact of existence. We say: 'the planet Mars exists' but not 'the planet Mars is'; and 'the quark exists even though it can't be seen' and not 'the quark is'. But this emphasis only hides a different usage of the word 'exist' which is not implied in the verb 'to be'.

Though it is a fact that we exist, we cannot deduce from that fact the further statement that we are here to exist. How can we know that we are here to exist? What kinds of proof or evidence would enable us to be certain about this statement? We are here because we are here is about as far as can get in proving this statement (see below for more on this in the ancillary answer 'We are here'). And there is no evidence that we can point to beyond our own existence which indicates that we are here to exist. We simply exist, and that is all we seem to know about this.

Treating it as one thing:

This answer would be treated monistically if it were possible to make it the solitary reason for one's living. But that seems to imply a state of catatonic inertia. Even meditating Buddhists are not simply existing for existing's sake. They exist to meditate and presumably to reach Nirvana. Besides, existence is not a predicate. It does not describe anything nor does it add anything to a sentence in which it is used. Existence is indeed a puzzle but it is not puzzling to say that we exist. Moreover, this answer may also be taken to extremes when it leads to the ancillary answer 'We are here because we are here' as mentioned below.

Treating it as one among many:

From a pluralistic point of view, there can be little objection to this answer as a reason for living. We do in fact exist; any doubts about it can only be impractical, metaphysical quibbling, best left to Cartesian doubters. The point is that we might as well do something with that existence. Thus, this answer can become a prelude to using other answers to the problem of living. By itself, this answer is vacuous but its assertion is a prerequisite to doing something positive with one's existence. Such is the elementary nature of this answer that it can be linked up with practically all the following answers. Or at least it is not incompatible or inconsistent with any of them. Being here to be or exist may be predicated with practically any verb, adjective, adverb or noun that one cares to think of.

Putting it into practice:

The above discussion suggests that this answer is difficult to put into practice. It is difficult to know what can be achieved if it could be put into practice. The answer fails to indicate what we exist for, therefore we cannot deduce from it what we can or should do in practice. There appears to be very little that we can do with this answer which would constitute putting it into practice. However, it may be interpreted as an assertion of beingness or existence. I am here and I exist, therefore I had better make the most of it. We need to get beyond this answer to get at the roots of our being. This takes us back to the *universal answers* discussed below since the roots of our being start with trying to understand why we are something rather than nothing.

Ancillary answers:

We are here. An even more elementary answer is simply to say "We are here". This expresses the fact of being without saying anything about it.

This is sometimes jokily extended to say "We're here because we're here because . . ." *ad infinitum*. But this also expresses a serious point about to elusiveness of a first cause or indeed of a final cause. The seriousness this view achieved prominence during the senseless First World War. The despairing soldier had no answer to make sense of insanities around him than to say that he was here because he was here. He had given up trying to make sense of how and why he got himself into such a vicious and vacuous conflict with an enemy he hardly ever saw. The saying was consequently expanded to infinity: "We're here because we're here because we're here . . . ." There was no sense in his being there at all therefore there was no point even thinking about it. This sentiment reflected the feelings of millions of soldiers who were caught up in that nightmare.

The 'To Do' Answer:
We are here to do or to act

What this answer means:
This answer means that our being able to do things and act in certain ways is the most important reason why we have being and existence. It can hardly be doubted that because we are capable of moving our limbs and other parts of our bodies, we can do things and act in certain ways. However, it seems superfluous to say that we are here to do nothing but do or act because this is what we do anyway. It goes without saying that we do things and act in certain ways. The fact of doing or acting is not at all interesting unless we are specify what we are doing or why we are acting and what we doing these things for.

What this answer is good for:
This answer at least reminds us that we are essentially active, doing creatures. We are not built simply to sit around doing nothing or to contemplate our navels. As animals we have evolved to be active and not to vegetate. Because of our language and conceptual powers we are also active mentally as well as physically. In doing and acting, we exercise both our bodies and the mental faculties that control bodily functions and abilities. Most of our thinking is directed towards taking action of some sort, either in the present or at some point in the future. Thus, this answer is good for drawing our attention to the importance of doing and acting in our lives. It makes us think about their particular role in our lives, regardless of what we actually doing or what we are acting for.

What's wrong with it:

It is wrong to emphasise doing and acting as if there were nothing more to life than being active. The bodily functions and mental faculties benefit as much from rest as from activity. There is nothing wrong with being lazy and languorous from time to time. Though we evolved as active animals even animals are not always rushing around all the time. There is a need for rest and lassitude if only to give the muscles a rest. Similarly, we don't need to be mentally active all the time. Our brains need rest and diversion as much as the rest of our bodies. There is also no persuasive proof or evidence that we are here to do or to act. We can only argue that we are capable of acting or doing therefore we have the possibility of doing so. But that doesn't prove that we are here to do or to act. Doing and acting are not complete synonyms. You can act something but not do it in the sense of going through the motions. But acting usually implies doing of some sort. I might do some cycling but I am not acting it, though I would be acting it if I only pretended to do the cycling. But the **act** of cycling does involve doing it. Thus, acting usually involves a degree of intention and deliberation which goes beyond mere doing.

Treating it as one thing:

This answer is particularly favoured by hyperactive workaholics. It justifies or rationalises their compulsion to work unceasingly. They are always thinking about what they have to do next. In that state of mind, it feels sinful to sit or lay around doing nothing. There is of course nothing wrong with that state of mind from a moral point of view. We are concerned about the harm that the state of mind might do to the individual afflicted with it. It is a state of mind that believes in action for action's sake. Thus, Sir Walter Scott puts the following words into the mouth of the Grand Master of the Knights Templar in his novel of the 12th century, *The Talisman:* "*Yet* and *but* are words for fools; wise men neither hesitate nor retract—they resolve and they execute." Wisdom, according to that view, means resolute action. It does not involve the careful consideration of all the pros and cons of action and the consequences of one's actions are not worth paying much attention to. Such deliberate thoughtlessness may have contributed to the downfall of the Knights Templar, a century or so later. On the other hand, this is the mentality of the businessman as well as the warrior. They both need to get things done quickly therefore they must rely on their intuitive grasp of affairs. The introspective hesitation of a Hamlet is out of place here. As Samuel Johnson put it: "Nothing will ever be attempted, if all possible objections must be first overcome." (*Rasselas*, Ch. VI, Penguin edition, p. 52)

Treating it as one among many:

This answer can be taken up by us all because we are basically practical animals who need to be doing things or, at least, seen to be doing things. But we don't need to be doing things all the time. We are just as potentially a lazy species as an active one. Therefore it is not the case that we are only here to do things or to be active all the time. Doing nothing at all is an entirely honourable profession for which we are all eminently skilled and qualified. This answer is more limited than the previous one in its possible links with other answers. It is limited to answers which imply activity of some kind.

Putting it into practice:

This answer is so uninformative that we are always putting it into practice, whether we are aware of it or not. When we do anything or act in any way we are putting this answer into practice by virtue of the way that we behave. We are implicitly recognising that our lives involve doing and acting. To put this answer explicitly and consciously into practice requires that we become acting and doing persons *per se*. But this is means that the answer tends towards a monistic treatment and makes it difficult to treat it pluralistically. This is however an inevitable result of the simplicity and uninformativeness of the answer.

Ancillary answers:

We are here to do nothing. This answer at least expresses our basic laziness. It is quite human for us to loll around doing nothing whatsoever. Doubtless it is good for us to do so from time to time. However, to make a philosophy of life out of this answer is hardly worth of us. It is enjoyable to do things and we typically get bored doing nothing at all. Indeed, if we don't find something to do there are always people around who will willingly tell us what to do. Laziness breeds busyness and *vice versa*. The two extremes go together very well.

We are here to do something or other. This merely extends the answer without specifying anything in particular. At least it implies doing something rather than nothing at all. But the choices lying before us are by no means narrowed. There is no end to what we could or could not do with our lives and, at one time or another during our lives, we are all looking for specific answers and cannot be content with such vague ones.

We are here to do what we like. This extends the answer in a hedonistic direction which is covered below under the heading of *solipsistic responses*.

The 'To Have' Answer:
We are here to have or to hold

What this answer means:

This answer means making the possession or holding of things, people, or ideas the mainstay of our existence. We typically live to take possession of things and hold on to them. To have or possess things is to make them a part of oneself. They belong to oneself and therefore bolster one's ego to a greater or lesser extent. In this frame of mind, we assume that the things that we possess and hold to our breasts are what make life worth living for. Nothing else but the having and holding of things seems to make sense of our lives.

What this answer is good for:

This answer is good in so far as the having and holding of things helps us to develop our personalities and make more of ourselves. We enrich our lives and add something to ourselves by possessing things. It isn't just the material objects that we possess but also what the objects mean to us, how they can be used, how they change our lives by having and holding them. Thus, the answer is good for helping us to make the most of our lives by using material and other possessions to add to our enjoyment and appreciation of life and its possibilities. The answer is also good for drawing our attention to the importance of these activities of having and holding regardless of what it is that we have or hold.

What's wrong with it:

In having and holding things there is the danger that they take possession of us and lessen us in the process. Even if there were nothing wrong with having or holding things it is still wrong to make too much out of doing so when we have no good reason to. For we are then giving them an importance which is unrealistic or inappropriate. When they become sacred to us or acquire a sentimental value over and above any material value, we are making more of them than can be realistically justified. There is also a narrowness about possessing things for its own sake. Such materialism is all too pervasive in our society. We constrict ourselves and enslave ourselves to things instead of using them to liberate our spirit and enrich our lives. And of course we do so by making them means to ends rather than ends in themselves.

Treating it as one thing:

When a person finds an extreme enjoyment in the possession and power of over objects, he or she will find that this answer not only is attractive but also makes sense of their lives. It is an answer not only of possessive materialists but also of most of us living in contemporary society. The love of shopping, of buying things, and of owning things is symptomatic of our being subservient to this answer to the problem of living. Materialism means seeing nothing else in life but the material objects that lie before us. We are being merely material persons when we place little or no value on unseen things such as ideas, art, music, scientific insights, academic matters, spirituality, and the like. Materialism for its own sake is undoubtedly a narrow frame of mind. But it is a very fashionable and compelling frame of mind that is not easily superseded or supplemented. Thus, the difficulty lies in convincing people that there is more to life than being merely materialistic.

Treating it as one among many:

We can make this answer a part of our lives without being the whole of our lives by cultivating thought, artistic appreciation, enjoyment of exercise, fresh air and scenery, and everything that belongs to everyone or no one. There is enjoyment in the possession of things but it is only one joy among innumerable which have nothing to do with possession at least in the material sense. Thus, this answer makes a lot of sense when it is balanced with other answers which cater for the non-material side of one's nature.

Putting it into practice:

This answer is equally uninformative in that we are continually putting it into practice every time we buy anything or take it into our possession. It is important however that we should be aware of what we are doing in having or holding anything. The act of doing so is too easily taken for granted and this happens when we are possessed by our possessing things rather than appreciating them for their own sakes. It is necessary to recognise when possessing things becomes a bad habit that needs to be tempered by other forms of activity. There is obviously more to life than the 'shop till you drop' mentality.

Ancillary answers:

We are here to have whatever we like. This also extends the answer in a hedonistic direction which is covered below under the heading of *Solipsistic Responses*.

We are here to have everything of beauty offered by the world. This answer is more or less dealt with in the *Aesthetic Answer* below.

What Can We Make Of These Answers?

On the face of it, very little can be made of these answers by themselves. We need to use them for something more, for some end or object beyond the mere activity implied by them, hence their possible religious significance as referred to above. Religious devotion bestows sanctity on mere existence, or on acts or things that have no other end except the significance given them by arbitrary religious acts or ceremonies. We can make something these answers only by supplementing them with other answers which add substance and direction to them. There is such mindlessness in these answers that they are not to be taken seriously but only considered as steps along the way towards fuller and better answers.

2
Universal Responses

➤   *The Existential Answer:* **We are here to be something rather than nothing.**

➤   *The Difference Answer:* **We are here to make a difference by the mere fact of having lived.**

➤   *The Maximal Answer:* **We are here to make the most of our lives.**

What's Universal About Them?

Universal responses are general and non-specific responses which have wide-ranging consequences. They apply not only to human beings but also to life as a whole and ultimately to the universe as a whole. They apply as much to other intelligent life-forms as to ourselves. And this includes possible life-forms in the universe which are totally alien to us. Because they are living beings like us, alien life-forms must also be faced with the same problems concerning the content of their lives. This follows from the fact of living which involves the problem of what to do with the gift of life. Every life-form will be faced with the universal problem of what to do with their lives, even if they lack language and intelligence by which to verbalise their concerns.

These answers concern the effects of our existence on the universe as a whole. They make us wonder whether it would make any difference at all whether we lived or died. In so wondering, our thoughts are elevated beyond everyday concerns to consider the significance of our lives from a universal point of view. Unless we make that kind of effort, it is certain that our lives will not amount to much in our own eyes. These answers encourage us to be more hopeful and to take a positive view of our lives when we take the wider perspective which these answers offer.

These reasons for living also help us to see that the universe as a whole is different in some discernible way because we have lived. It is only from a strictly materialist point of view that it can be argued that our existence makes no difference at all to the universe because of its physical vastness. But these answers make the point that the universe is more than just an agglomeration of matter contained in limitless time and space. It contains also life-forms who can make what they will of the universe's content, provided they possess the knowledge and technology sufficient to achieve their ends. As also mentioned in the *Introduction* above, these answers are supported by our knowledge of the structure and development of the universe. We can arrive at them rationally by appealing to empirical evidence concerning the way that we have emerged from the physical, chemical and biological processes of the universe.

The Existential Answer:
We are here to be something rather than nothing

What this answer means:
Here the verb 'to be' acquires an object, namely, 'something' which is to be contrasted with 'nothing'. What the 'something' is for each of us to decide for ourselves. It is the ultimate variable 'x' in the algebraic formulae of life. The notion of nothing has been unending problem to philosophers ever since Parmenides proclaimed that it did not exist. How can one possibly think of nothing? To be thinking at all means thinking about something even if it can't be brought to mind. If something really is nothing at all then it can't be thought of. Yet we have a notion of it in the absence of something or everything, as Sartre argued. When we are sitting waiting for a friend in a cafe and he or she doesn't turn up then we are aware of that absence. We know when nothing has occurred when we expect something to occur. Nothing can only be a description of the absence of something and therefore only exists in relation to something.

This is called the 'existential' answer not because of any deliberate links with existential philosophy but because it is concerned the basic fact of our existence by which we are something rather than nothing. The fact that we know of that existence is significant in itself. Such knowledge can be used by us to do the best we can as a collective species. We apparently do not have that knowledge of our existing for nothing. When asked 'What is a miracle?', Einstein is supposed to have replied 'What is not a miracle?' This correctly illustrates the fact that being something rather than nothing is a stupendously improbable event. Everything about our lives is truly miraculous and ultimately unaccountable. Nothing but mean-minded obtuseness can prevent anyone from seeing this fact and appreciating it to the full.

What this answer is good for:
This answer is good for reinforcing our confidence in the fact of our existence in relation to something else within that existence. It is not the fact that we exist which is important. It is what we exist for and in respect

of, which is important. We may have come into being entirely by chance but it does not follow that our lives amount to nothing when we have the possibility of doing something with those lives.

This is another example of an answer which we have in common with the universe itself. For the physical account of the origins of the universe suggests that it came into existence as something rather than nothing. The physical nature of the universe is such as to make something out of nothing. As far as we know the universe emerged from a 'singularity' which is as nearly being nothing as we are capable of grasping by thought. The initial conditions of the universe plus the events very early in its expansion have ensured that ever-increasing complexity of organisation and interaction has occurred throughout the universe. This presupposition cannot be proved by reference to the facts of the universe since these facts may be used to disprove this presupposition just as much as to prove it. We are free to interpret the facts either way. The activity of arguing each way is on-going and interminable. The challenge here is to argue on the positive side and thereby invite the negative response.

Our reasons for making the presupposition that we are here to be something rather than nothing lie not only in the structure of the universe but also in the way that we have been given time to do something with our lives. Time is a product of the expansion of the universe and we are constantly battling against the inexorable passage of time to get things done. In the course of time we all fall apart into our basic constituents. Everything that we accomplish in life flies in the face of this disintegration through time. We therefore add something to the universe which it is otherwise not organised to achieve. In this way, we defy the universe in our own very small way.

Though the universe is independent of us, we are intimately a part and product of it. There is a fruitful interaction occurring here in which we constantly assert our independence of the universe by doing what we can do as living beings. We are something rather than nothing because of our constant tussle with the universe to be something that universe itself cannot possibly be in so far as it is independent of us. In being something we therefore surpass the universe which is ultimately nothing in itself since only we are capable of making something of it.

What's wrong with it:

It is wrong to make too much of being something when one can be quite content being a complete nonentity. There can be no definite proof that we are here to be something rather than nothing. It may suit our purposes to argue that we are something or it may not, depending on the point that we are making. This answer is also deficient in its lack of informativeness. We still have the problem of what the 'something' is supposed to mean. How can we judge what is 'something' and what is not? And even when we arrive at something, how can we tell that this particular something is what we are looking for? This answer therefore raises more questions and problems than it answers.

Treating it as one thing:
The idea that one has to be something rather than nothing can fuel a person's ambitions. It can be interpreted to mean that we have to be somebody in order to be something. Thus, we seek fame or notoriety in trying to be somebody. It can also be taken to neurotic and even psychopathic extremes when the individual aspires to megalomania. There is no need to strive single-mindedly to be something when one can also learn to be content being a nobody or a nonentity. There is equally as much to be said for being nothing as for being something (see the *Ancillary Answers* below for more on this).

Treating it as one among many:
This answer helps us to cope with the horrible feeling that we have come into the world apparently to be nothing at all and that it doesn't really matter whether we were born or not for all the difference our lives will make on the world. There is more to life than worrying all the time about our cosmic worthlessness. Also, the answer is insufficient because we need to know what the 'something' means. The blanks have to be filled in, preferably by reference to the other answers to the problem of life and living, some of which are listed in this book.

Putting it into practice:
In putting this answer into practice we are at least trying to do something with our lives. For doing something means that what we do has some meaning for us, therefore it must be more than nothing. We put this answer into practice by constantly exercising our judgments, tastes and discernment to recognise the ways in which we are in fact something or can be if we so choose. In short, by behaving as if there is something in life rather than nothing we are putting this answer into practice.

Ancillary answers:
We are here to be nothing. This answer is related to the above one in that it is its negation (and it to be distinguished from the above ancillary answer

'We are here to do nothing'). There is possibly as much to be said in favour of this answer as the above one. But it is so negative and depressing that we can be forgiven for dismissing it as being not worthy of self-respecting human beings. Yet both saints and murderers have made a lot of this answer. The former use this answer to justify their being completely self-abnegating and life-denying in their behaviour. The latter use it to justify murder or any kind of anti-social act because nothing matters if we are nothing and therefore moral restrictions don't matter either.

We are here by pure, blind chance. This is particularly the answer of biologists who take their own science to its logical conclusion and who exclude purposefulness from the universe entirely, even though they will acknowledge that the living beings behave in a purposeful, goal-seeking manner. It is however a quite informative answer. Our lives are full of chance. Everything we do can meet with good or bad fortune. Life is a lottery. But that is not what is important about life. What is important is making the most of any chances that life has to offer.

We are here to help rebuild the unity of the universe which first existed at its beginning. This answer gives an overall end to human activities. It is however unsupported by any clear scientific evidence. It is more like wishful thinking than a realistic answer to the question of why we are here. Furthermore, the notion of 'unity of the universe' is easily but wrongly identified with God. This is wrong because that unity consists of nothing more than the material universe, the initial conditions, and the physical laws that have governed its development since its beginning. We contribute to this unified rebuild by our making sense of our activities in terms of higher unities. We also contribute by staving off our own dissolution through time and by thereby maintaining our unity and integrity.

The Difference Answer:
We are here to make a difference by the mere fact of having lived

What this answer means:
Making a difference means adding something to the sum-total of things that have not existed before in quite the same way. It means that the life of even the most insignificant human being makes a difference because of the interactions of that person with other people and because of what that person has done during his or her lifetime. Thus, the differences made by our having lived at all consist in the effect that we have had on other

people and the things that we have done during our lifetime.

The fact of having lived implies that something can be done with one's life, however trivial or inconsequential. Life involves doing purposeful things. Popping a grape into one's mouth is purposeful though fairly languid act. But it makes a big difference to the grape which finds itself being chewed up and consumed by digestive juices. Moreover, this act of grape popping may seem to be an entirely inconsequential act as far as the big, wide universe is concerned. But the exact significance of any event occurring anywhere in the universe cannot be calculated by any scientific theory, as has been shown by the recent formulation of chaos theory. There is simply no end to the ramifications of any event in the universe. Its repercussions recede far into infinity, as in the case of the Mandelbrot set, whose bottom can never be reached.

This answer might also be called the 'evolutionary' answer because evolution implies that an accumulation of differences between species of living beings occurs over a long period of time. Thus, from an evolutionary point of view, we may be said to be contributing to this accumulation of differences when we develop our own way of living and doing things. 'Evolutionary' also implies a struggle for existence and a struggle to ascertain the fact of our presence in this indifferent universe. Unless we struggle to justify our place in the universe, there is little point in our being here at all. Making a discernible difference by what we do in life is at least the beginning of justifying our existence in the here and now.

Differences are also made by the processes of the universe in creating distinctive entities that emerge with unpredictable properties. The complexity of living creatures enables them to create more complex differences than existed previously. And intelligent beings have the ability to create even more complex differences because of the complexity of their cultural activities. The differences that we make are contributing to those which the universe makes anyway, whether we were here or not. But being physically different is not enough for we need to know why there are differences of any kind at all and just why they are considered differences. In other words, we want to know and understand why things are as they are, which leads us to the *Scientific Responses* mentioned below.

What this answer is good for:
This answer is good for encouraging us to make more of ourselves than just doing the obvious things such as eating, drinking, sleeping and having sex. We are all capable of doing extraordinary things which are more valuable and worthwhile than we may think to be the case. Perhaps the best

antidote to the thought that our lives may be for nothing and the best vindication of this answer's value is the celebrated film, *It's A Wonderful Life*. In this feature film, James Stewart plays a character who is given a chance by an angel to experience what his town would have been like if he had never lived. No doubt, the film exaggerates greatly the extent to which one person's non-existence can make a difference. Nevertheless, it is arguable that there would discernible differences to the lives of other people if any one of us had failed to be born.

What's wrong with it:

One might ask what difference does it make whether one makes a difference or not? What does it matter? What does anything matter? Why should we be here to make a difference? The answer assumes that which needs to be proven and possibly it never can be proven. It is also deficient in not making clear what a 'difference' is and why it is of such importance. Anyone can choose to call an activity or lifestyle different for whatever reason that they dream up. A new way of killing people would make a difference, so that we need a way of making moral distinctions concerning the value or lack of value of differences. Also there is a lack of criteria by which we can reach agreement about what is or is not different. There is less difficult as far as the objects of perception are concerned. But it is cultural differences which this answer particularly concerns. Too many differences between us make it difficult for us to live comfortably with each other.

Treating it as one thing:

Cultivating our differences from other people can lead to increasing alienation from our fellow beings. Our similarities to other people can be more important because they enable us to empathise with people and work with them more easily. In any case, it may not be enough to make a difference by the mere fact of having lived. There has to be more to life than that. Our differences ought to be constructive and positive by adding to the sum-total of things. We may in fact enjoy or profit from being exactly the same as other people. An individual may be content to emulate other people and not see any merit in standing out at all.

Treating it as one among many:

The importance of this answer lies in the fact that our most trivial actions can make a difference even though they may seem trivial and inconsequential to ourselves. We don't have to be assessing our actions all the time to convince ourselves that we are making a difference. We are making a difference anyway. The question is whether the difference that we are making really matters to ourselves. For that reason, this answer is insufficient in itself to meet our needs in making the best sense of our lives.

The mere fact of having lived is sufficient in itself to encourage us to make something of our lives. We all have a whole lifetime which we are fortunate enough to have both behind and before us. This implies that we can at any stage look at our lives as a whole and assess them accordingly. We can judge whether we could have done more with our lives and whether we can do more in the future. This way of looking at our lives enables us to pinpoint the ways in which we have made a difference.

Putting it into practice:

This is put into practice when we review our actions, thoughts and decisions, and make a judgment concerning whether these have in fact made a difference. The above discussion suggests that we have to make up our own minds as whether we have made difference or not. We need not rely on others to make that judgment though it is obviously gratifying when they assert that we have made a difference.

Ancillary answers:

We are here to make a difference. This answer obviously abbreviates the main one above. In so doing it is less informative. It is also comparable with an additional ancillary answer: 'we are here to be different'. The two are distinguishable in that the former is more pro-active, general and universal whereas the latter more circumscribed, social and culture-bound. Making a difference means doing something whereas one can be different without doing anything. Any deed or thought at all may be construed as making a difference, but not every deed or thought can be deemed to make a difference to one's life.

The Maximal Answer:
We are here to make the most of our lives

What this answer means:

Perhaps it is not enough to make a difference by the mere fact of having lived. We should also make the most of our lives by doing everything we can reasonably and ethically think of doing. Making the most of our lives means doing everything worthwhile with our lives that we can think of. We make more of ourselves by adding something to them which did not exist before. We do so by learning something new, visiting a new country, making a new friend or whatever.

This answer is called 'maximal' because you can hardly do more with your life than make the most of it. The greatest quantity of identifiable things which you do with your life is surely the maximum that can be expected. You can't do more than the most. However, at any particular point in time, you can do more than you are doing at the moment. Therefore, as you live your life you can add to it by doing more and more and accomplishing more and more. That at any rate is an ideal to be striven for.

What this answer is good for:

This answer tell us that living is not a simple, one-off process and that there is more to life than simply living aimlessly from day to day doing everyday, humdrum things. We have the opportunity to make the most of our lives by the fact of living but only *we* can do this. We cannot rely on others to make sure that we live our lives to the full. We are alone responsible for having done as much as we can with our lives. Those who blame their shortcomings on their parents, their upbringing or unfavourable events are usually making excuses for not having done as much as they could have. There are invariably many other people in the world who have not been deterred by much more formidable disadvantages in their lives.

What's wrong with it:

It is wrong to think that making the most of our lives is necessarily a good or laudable thing. We may be rushing around getting nowhere and achieving nothing. We may be doing thoroughly bad and evil things with our lives. The quality of what is being done is therefore important. Again, one can ask why it matters that anyone should make the most of themselves. How can we possibly know that we are here to make the most of ourselves? It is a matter of personal opinion what constitutes making the most of one's life. We can arbitrarily decide that we have made the most of our opportunities even though there is no evidence to support that view and no one agrees with us.

Treating it as one thing:

This answer, pursued on its own, leads to our making too much of life and to our becoming neurotic and over-anxious about any opportunities that we may have missed. If we make too much of life then we may be let down in our expectations. We should take life seriously but not too seriously. When it is made into an end in itself the thought that we are here to make the most of our lives can be taken to undesirable extremes. 'A rolling stone gathers no moss' is a proverb that is applicable here. It may be better to stick to one or a few things in our lives rather than trying to cram too many things into it. In any case, we usually end up constructing our own shells within which we feel secure. Breaking out of that shell may make life worse and more unbearable instead of enriching it as this answer assumes.

Treating it as one among many:

Trying to do everything that we can possibly think of doing is not only tiring but a limitless burden on the soul. There can be end to such fervent striving to make the most of life. We deserve to give ourselves a break from time to time. Making the most of life needs to be linked with other answers to make sense of it. Unless we are clear in our minds what will make more of our lives then it can be only a random groping around which wastes our opportunities in life instead of making something of it.

Putting it into practice:

This answer is put into practice when we review our activities and think about whether we have done as much with our time and opportunities as we could have done. If we consider the quality of our activities to be important then it is necessary to cultivate our judgment and discernment to make sure that we are making the most of our lives for the best possible reasons and with best possible results. Making the most of our lives therefore involves increasing the quality of our lives just as much it involves filling it with as many activities as possible.

Ancillary answers:

We are here to work and play as hard as we can. This answer helps us to narrow the field down. We are not just to live life to the full, we are also to work and play to the utmost. But it is not the whole answer as there ought to be room in our lives for doing nothing at all. As the poet puts it: "What is this life if full of care, we have no time to stand and stare." (Davies) "They also serve who only stand and wait." (Milton) The Buddhists also have much to say on the matter, mainly on the contemplative side.

What Can We Make Of These Answers?

The point of these answers is that we can make as much or as little of them as we want. They are the most general humanistic answers that might be thought of. They encourage people to make as much of their lives as possible without specifying the ways in which they might do so. They may induce existential angst in the process. We understandably fear the freedom of choice they offer because of the responsibility on us to make the best possible judgments. In doubting our capacity to make the best choices, we are strengthened as individuals. The doubt makes us think more about the problems we face instead of blundering blindly into things. And we learn by experience to make the most of the freedoms which are bestowed on each of us.

3
Religious Responses

> *The Theological Answer:* **We are here to worship God.**
> *The Meditative Answer:* **We are here to contemplate eternity.**
> *The Humanist Answer:* **We are here to serve humanity.**

What's Religious About Them?

These answers are religious in that the first is concerned with the worship of God, the second with a religious regard to significance of eternity and the third with a religious devotion to humanity. They are religious because they elevate their objects and give them dogmatic and static significance. God, eternity and humanity are transformed and made sacred and transcendent. They are adored and ritualised beyond all everyday, physical objects. This applies even to the humanist answer which inevitably makes more of humanity in place of supernatural entities, and maybe to excess.

A religious answer is usually contrasted with the scientific view of the universe and our place in it. Religion is renowned for taking a dogmatic stance concerning what life and the universe is all about. It wishes to remove doubt and uncertainty by making a virtue of uncritical belief. It relies on faith and past authority rather than on the painstaking search for evidence which characterises scientific endeavour. For that reason, religion is usually seen to be incompatible with science. However, science has grown out of religion and ought eventually to supersede it. How it may do so is presently uncertain.

The Theological Answer:
We are here to worship God

What this answer means:

This answer means that the purpose of our existence is to serve God because we have been created by God to serve God's purposes. We have no choice in the matter because God is a superior being, and because God knows what is best for us. But this is all on the assumption that there is a God and that the universe has been made to suit the purposes of a superior being. It has long been acknowledged by religious people that the belief in God is a matter of personal revelation than on any evidence supported by science or observation for that matter. This reduces the notion of God to a crutch on which emotionally and intellectually deprived people lean because they lack the inner strength to live in a universe that is not dominated by a superior being looking after them. This is the theory of God as fairy godmother who is waiting in the wings to make everything right for them.

What this answer is good for:

This answer is good for individuals who have a genuine belief in the existence of God in whatever form. However, it also the resort of those who cannot live with the world as it is but who need to hypothesise the existence of a superior being on whom to pin all their hopes. It helps those who need dependence more than independence in their lifestyles. It is also good for superstitious people who imagine that there are influences underlying everyday incidents which we cannot perceive as we can only speculate about them. Aliens, angels, spirits, and stars (through astrology) are examples of the kind of influences thought to be at work there.

What's wrong with it:

This answer is deficient because the existence of God can never be proved to the satisfaction of any sceptic who has never had the benefit of personal revelation. And what does it matter whether God exists or not? Does the existence of God really make the slightest difference to anyone's life, even when they believe in it most fervently? It is no more than cotton wool in which people wrap themselves to protect them from the coldness of a godless reality. It is arguable that the belief alone may be making all the difference but the actual existence itself makes no difference. The history of humankind suggests that it is better to believe in something rather than nothing but to be sincere and proof against all argument it has to be the best belief which one can possibly strive for. In the face of what science is telling us about ourselves and the universe, God belief is no longer sufficient. We need better reasons for believing in ourselves.

Treating it as one thing:

God intoxicated people may find solace in this answer and may accordingly devote their lives to the worship of God. "God meant me to do this" can be a justification for the most horrendous forms of human behaviour e.g. shooting or bombing people or going to war for spurious reasons. In such circumstances, one man's God is another man's Devil. At the other extreme, people identify themselves with God to the extent of denying the needs of their bodies in order to mortify their souls. The resultant asceticism can only invite misery and a premature death with nothing to show at all for having lived.

Treating it as one among many:

It is possible to believe in God but not be dogmatic about it. This enables the believer to tolerate unbelief. Thus, both God belief and atheism are tolerated in a pluralistic culture which respects conflicting answers to questions of religion and different views of its role in society. A pluralistic society need not attempt to eradicate God belief or supersede it in any way. If the notion of God truly has no future then it will erode of its own accord. In the meantime, those who believe in God must acknowledge the personal nature of that belief which they cannot expect others to share.

Putting it into practice:

Putting this answer into practice means subordinating one's entire life and existence to this overbearing being. It presents the individual either with impossible choices or with no choices at all. Either God is an attainable goal that cripples the individual and ruins his self-confidence, or God is a demoralising crutch which robs the individual of self-reliance and self-respect. Far from inspiring people the notion of God often degrades them. Indeed, people can do the most devilish things in the name of God, for example, kill other people who believe in God because they have different views of God. In practice, astronomers have always had difficulty finding a place for God in the universe. When Napoleon wondered why the great astronomer Laplace failed to mention God in his books about the universe, he replied "Sire, I had no need of that hypothesis". It is indeed a dream thing that we can learn to live without and be the better for it.

Ancillary answers:

We are here to worship the Devil. This answer is obviously the antithesis of the main one which invites it by contrast. The elevation of a superior deity above us all invites the opposite view of a contrasting being which is the opposite of everything attributed to God. Devil worship is not possible unless one believes in the existence of some good God with which the Devil may be contrasted. Only an atheistic dualist view can save us from the Manichean dichotomy that divides the world rigidly into good and evil as if it were possible for these attributes to exist independently of us. Moreover, devil worship even today appeals to devious people who like to be different but merely marginalise themselves in the process.

The Meditative Answer:
We are here to contemplate eternity

What this answer means:

Contemplating eternity means disregarding the finite, ephemeral things of life in favour of that which is eternal and everlasting. This answer implies that the here-and-now is not the true reality since it is insignificant in the face of eternity. This reflects the ancient quest for absolute stability and reliability amid the shifting sands of external reality. The ancient Greeks sought that which is 'ageless and deathless' and resists the ravages of time and decay. In the face of changing circumstances over which we have no control, it is understandable that we should look for stable and reliable rocks in the shifting sands of events. This is where the desire for eternity arises. It is restful and reassuring in a world that is ever-changing and full of unpredictable and unexpected events.

What this answer is good for:

This answer is good for taking our thoughts beyond the here-and-now to dwell on the permanency of eternity in so far as anything can be everlasting. We exercise our imaginations and abstract faculties by transcending perceptual appearances to reach what seems to be behind and beyond such appearances. Thinking about eternity makes us realise how restricted our own lives are and how little significance those lives have in relation to the endlessness of eternity. It may also be good, from time to time, to take one's mind off the here-and-now and meditate on eternal things. But it is only good for a limited period of time since it is in the here-and-now that we must live our lives. The merit of this answer lies in its limited and circumscribed application and not its being way of life worthwhile in itself.

What's wrong with it:

This answer is wrong in that eternity can never be comprehended or reached by a mere human being. We can only *think* that we are contemplating it but thinking does not make it so. It leads to a Platonic frame of mind which despises perceptual reality in favour of a more permanent reality said to be behind perceptual reality. It makes us despair perhaps unnecessarily about the apparent insignificance of our lives within the limitless expanse of eternity. If life is an oasis in the midst of limitless eternity then the last thing that we are here to do is to contemplate eternity since it is the antithesis of life and living. The oasis must be cultivated and

Prolonged and not neglected in favour of an empty eternity that is meaningless and fruitless.

Treating it as one thing:

The meditative answer has been much popularised by eastern religions such as Buddhism. The monkish way of life may be harmless in itself as it threatens no one. But it is also unproductive and essentially antisocial because it takes the individual out of social circulation and deprives society of his or her contribution. It may be criticised as an out-of-date right hemispheric and non-verbal approach to life which even eastern nations are steadily abandoning in favour of the more complex Western way of thinking.

Treating it as one among many:

Solitude and meditation may be as good in moderation as they are bad in excess. Some meditation and solitude may be good for everyone, though it is entirely the choice of the individual as to the timing and length of such activities. Our social life might even improve if we learn to enjoy solitary contemplation on a regular but limited basis. There is much to be said for solitude as a means of developing one's inner being and of getting in touch with oneself. We need solitude and meditation to getting ourselves together as a whole. But this can only be one strategy among many in one's endeavour to make the most of one's life.

Putting it into practice:

This answer is put into practice when one's entire life is devoted to contemplation. It therefore needs to be shared with other answers unless the simplicity of a contemplative life is what the individual wants and needs. However, the monastic or ascetic life nowadays only makes sense as a withdrawal from the world in order to return to it refreshed and ready to participate in society more effectively and wholeheartedly than before. To do nothing but contemplate eternity is to be hardly living at all.

Ancillary answers:

We are here to meditate. This is both ancillary to and implied by the aforesaid answer. It is even more inadequate as a stand-alone reason for living than the above one as it has no object. It involves meditation for meditation's sake. Transcendental meditation, Buddhism and other eastern religions make a great deal of this. An absolute commitment to a meditative way of life means returning to the mindlessness of the womb.

Denying the self and all its desires, aspirations and emotions is not an advance but a retreat. It is a negation of life rather than an affirmation of life. It means running away from life's opportunities instead of embracing them. The laughs and smiles of the meditative devotee bespeak the vacant mind. He has no problems because he has decided not to have any by erasing his mind. Such empty-headedness is admirable in cows and sheep but not in human beings. The meditative way of life is far from being challenging and demanding. It is the easiest and least commendable way of life that we can give ourselves. It is too easy to wipe the slate clean and remain permanently empty. The hard thing is to face up to all the difficulties of life and still take time to laugh and smile whatever the adversities and setbacks

The Humanist Answer:
We are here to serve humanity

What this answer means:

We are all members of the human race by virtue of the fact that we are all human beings. We are born as human beings and die as human beings therefore in a sense what lies between these events belongs to humanity. For that reason, the principal means by which we express our humanity is by serving each other. To serve humanity means thinking about the welfare and future of human beings in general as well doing things for people in particular. However we choose to serve humanity has consequences for the whole human race as well as benefiting individuals. Doing something for another human being serves all humanity in a sense. Whatever one does for one's family and friends benefits humanity to a limited extent. This is because of the ramifications of our humane actions which spread out like the waves of disturbed pond. What little we do for others disseminates far beyond the act and has effects that we may never be aware of. For example, just the acts of smiling and saying good morning may lift the spirits of others and make their day more tolerable than otherwise.

What this answer is good for:

This answer is good for showing us the extent to which many of our actions do help to serve humanity even though it may not occur to us that this is the case. We must look to ourselves if we are to make any kind of progress or advancement in this universe. As a species, we need to get our own house in order so that we can begin to benefit the planet and other species instead of our own narrow commercial needs. Thus, serving humanity entails also serving life as a whole since our existence is dependent on life continuing on this planet. The food we eat and the air we breathe is provided by animals and plant life respectively.

What's wrong with it:

This answer is wrong in that there is much more to the universe than our paltry and insignificant species living on this miniscule speck of a planet. It is the height of arrogance to focus on humanity as if that were all that matters. In fact, the human race amounts to very little in the sum-total of things. Because our knowledge and understanding is strictly limited we cannot afford to magnify our sense of importance beyond all reason. In failing to think in terms of the welfare of the whole planet we merely continue its ruination and the devastation of the species on it.

Treating it as one thing:

Unspeakable cruelties may be performed on other people by those who think that the service of humanity is more important than the life and well-being of a single human being. The notion of humanity, like any other high ideal, may be used to justify wicked and unjust acts. Totalitarian states often justify their inhumanities on that basis. They think that the lives of individuals must be sacrificed for the greater good of the whole. This is making the idea of humanity more important than the individual human being. This is a top-down view whereas the bottom-up view focuses on the individual. Thus, the answer to this problem is to ensure that the service of humanity is limited to practical goods and benefits. Particular individuals must benefit from this service and it is not just an idea enforced arbitrarily. In other words, the welfare and benefit of the individual human being is paramount over any ideology or state-led policies.

This humanist answer is implied in the works of religious people even though they pay lip service to the view that they are serving God. The fact is that in the act of serving God they often serve humanity in the process. Also, from a religious point of view, this answer only substitutes humanity for God as an object of worship and religious devotion. This was certainly the approach of Auguste Comte who attempted to establish a religion of humanity in the nineteenth century. His attempt failed because he was making idol of humanity so that his religion was Catholicism by another name. There is more about Comte in my book, *The Answer Lies Within us* (Ashgate Publishing, 1998), page 11.

Treating it as one among many:

Merely by being sociable individuals we are serving humanity. As the *Sociable Answers* show, we contribute to the wellbeing of the human race by being nice, co-operative, competitive and interacting individuals. Thus, there is no need to make a religion out of something that we all do when we behave ourselves as human beings. We benefit humanity without having to think that we are doing so. We feed the hungry of the world because we empathise with their plight and not because we are benefiting humanity. The humanist answer is a way of understanding what we do anyway, whatever we call it. It is no more than a description which has its uses like any other description.

Putting it into practice:

We put this answer into practice when we devote our time, thoughts and energies to benefiting *other* people. We give added meaning to our beneficent acts because we are not just doing them for selfish reasons or to appease our own feelings of guilt or inadequacy. Whether we are conscious of doing so or not, these acts benefit humanity, as they are abstract acts of benevolence and we never meet or know of the individuals who are benefiting from them.

The dangers of putting this answer into practice arise from treating humanity as an end which is more important than any one individual. The result of doing so is justify the sacrifice and even killing of individuals in the name of this ideal. If millions die in the course of improving agricultural practice or in making village life the basis of civilisation, humanity is not served but debased in the process, even it is thought that humanity will benefit in the long run. When Henry Ford benefited humanity by introducing a universal car for all and by improving the working conditions for all, it was done specifically by benefiting individuals. It was a bottom-up revolution rather than a top-down one. Government didn't come into it as it was begun by relatively small company which came up with the right principles at the right time and, as a result, the consumer revolution of the 20th century was set in motion.

Ancillary answers:

We are here to do our duty. This ancillary answer makes a duty out of our service to humanity as it invariably means doing things for the benefit of other people on a formal basis. It is impossible to have a duty unless there is a social or cultural context within which it is conceived to be a duty. The duty of parents towards their children, the duty of an employer towards his employees, the duty of a politician towards his constituents; these are all social obligations that are meaningless outside the context of parenthood, employer/employee relations, and the political sphere, respectively. These contexts provide the formal basis on which each duty relies for its rules and obligations. Furthermore, all these contexts combine to form the overall context of the human race and its aims and aspirations. Thus, the formal basis relates ultimately to the abstract needs of humanity as opposed to the concrete needs of individuals. This answer was particularly favoured by Kant who did more than anyone to make the 19th century a duty-bound century. Several generations of people spent restless nights worrying whether they had done their duty during the previous day and whether they would be able to do their duty the next day. The question is to what extent it is our duty to think of the plight of the human race.

What Can We Make Of These Answers?

One needs to be religious minded to make anything of these answers. Even the humanist answer requires a religious regard for humanity in the abstract. The question is whether being religious minded is an out-of-date state of mind or not. Do these choices impede the individual's ability to make as much as they might of the complex society in which they live? I would argue that they do. It is not the case that advances in scientific knowledge have made religions irrelevant. What will make religion irrelevant are advances in understanding and appreciating our own self-image. We need confidence in what we can or cannot do as a species. In other words, confidence in our own abilities to see the way forward and do what is best not only for ourselves as a species but also as caretakers of this planet. Thus, the ecological and other answers can make it unnecessary for religion to have such a paralysing hold on people's minds and feelings as it presently has.

4
Philosophical Responses

- ➢ *The Philosophy Answer:* **We are here to philosophise about everything**
- ➢ *The 'Meaning' Answer:* **We are here to discover the meaning of life**
- ➢ *The Stoical Answer:* **We are here to put up with the vicissitudes of fortune**

What's Philosophical About Them?

These answers are philosophical in that they represent philosophical ways of thinking and living. They consist in applying philosophy in everyday life and for everyday purposes. The word 'philosophical' in this context refers to an inquiring and questioning attitude of mind which transcends the mundane and commonplace to find more significance in things than is given by means of perception. Philosophical tools and techniques are used to help us answer questions which concern the nature of things, what life is all about, and how to deal stoically with whatever life has to fling at us. An interest in philosophical subjects can lead a person to consider everything in the light of philosophy whether or not they achieve enlightenment by so doing.

The philosophical view is therefore one of detachment and pondering on life, often to the extent of not quite belonging to the society in which one lives. The philosophically inclined person is often assumed to be an impractical dreamer but the opposite can be the case. The philosophical standpoint can enable the individual to be more realistic and down-to-earth than the average person because they do not allow themselves to be carried away by adverse circumstances or by irrational treatment from others. That standpoint is open-minded and self-critical. Thus, things are seen as they are and other people are seen as they are, because philosophically inclined persons are more critical of their own thinking and less easily carried away by feelings and circumstances. They don't allow themselves to be carried away by extreme feelings, and retain a balanced view of the world. This is because they have developed their inner being to a greater extent than other people and are less inclined to allow their emotions to get the better of them. There is more on the notion of inner being and its strength in my book, *Advancing Humanity: The Need to Make Our Own Future* (2016), on pages 68-85.

The Philosophy Answer:
We are here to philosophise about everything

What this answer means:
This answer means that we are here to use philosophy to make sense of everything in our lives. It means making a way of life out of philosophy and the application of philosophical tools and techniques. These tools and techniques range from simple verbalising and the avoidance of self-contradiction, all the way to the conceptual and logical analysis of problems. Above all, they involve questioning and criticising everything to try and get to the root or bottom of things. These tools and techniques are used to direct thought upon whatever words, feelings, modes of behaviour, situations which one comes across in daily life. There is nothing in life that cannot be a subject for philosophical inquisition.

What this answer is good for:
This answer is good for making philosophers of us all. In so far as we need to be more thoughtful and considerate persons, philosophising can help us in that direction. Everyone capable of talking for themselves can also philosophise for themselves. We should not take everything that happens on its face value. It pays us to get below the surface and find inner meanings and connections which escape superficial scrutiny. In this way we confront realities and find ways of making sense of them and then or coping with them through science and technology.

What's wrong with it:
It is wrong to think that we can solve our problems merely by philosophising about everything. It does no more than encourage armchair theorising to the extent that people no longer act decisively according to their inclinations and instincts. Too much reasoning cripples action and stultifies feelings and impulses. Philosophy takes us into the realm of abstractions and away from the directness and immediacy of plain common sense. It is wrong to make too much of abstract thought because it dehumanises us and makes think that ideas are more important than people and their feelings and concerns.

Treating it as one thing:
To treat philosophising as the one thing worth living for is to make a profession out of armchair theorising. Thinking about things cannot solve

all our problems. It can only contribute ways of coping with them. Philosophy by itself can achieve nothing in the long term but perpetuate uncertainty, puzzlement and bewilderment. A person who is nothing but a philosopher will never interact with other people as they are too wrapped up in their own thoughts and ideas. They need to get out more and forget about their philosophy from time to time.

Treating it as one of many:

Philosophising can play a worthy part in a well balanced life-style when it is used appropriately and with moderation. Philosophy is undoubtedly part of the answer to the problem of living. We need it to complete our lives and to learn to live within ourselves. It enables us to make much more of life than the merely here and now. The significance of trivial things is enhanced because much more thought and consideration can be put into them. Philosophy should not be regarded as something only for a clever and well-educated elite. Everyone can philosophise who can handle abstract terms and say meaningful things about philosophical topics such what is mind etc. It has been shown that children as soon as they master language are able to formulate philosophical questions about life and living. It is regrettable that adults often lose their philosophical curiosity, cease to question things and become dull dogmatists.

Putting it into practice:

We put this answer into practice not only by attending philosophy courses or by reading works of philosophy but also by philosophising for ourselves. The formal learning of philosophy should be supplemented by thinking out things for oneself and this is best done in group philosophising sessions in which there is free and open conversation and discussion about philosophical matters. Philosophy cafés are an important way of bringing philosophy to the public. Also, the education system should provide for philosophy for children so that they do not lose their natural propensity to question and inquire into things.

Ancillary answers:

We are here to be philosophers and thinkers: This answer differs in emphasis from the above one because it refers to the profession of philosophy rather than just the act of philosophising. We can all benefit from philosophising but it is less certain that we can all benefit from becoming philosophers and thinkers. Traditionally, only the best brains are allowed to be philosophers and thinkers as such. The rest are liable to become no more than philosophasts, pseudo-intellectuals, poseurs, dilettantes, and the like. Thus, we are not all cut out to be philosophers and thinkers who are capable of understanding philosophical problems to an academic level. But nevertheless we are all philosophers in so far as we all have a philosophy of life. There is more on the problem of defining what philosophers are in the Introduction to my book: *What is Philosophy* (Dunedin Academic Press, 2008).

The 'Meaning' Answer
We are here to discover the meaning of life

What this answer means:
The meaning of life consists in what we can say about life in general and about our own lives in particular. Discovering the meaning of life requires us to find out what we ourselves believe to be its meaning, both in general and in particular. Life in general has a meaning for us because we can treat it as a general conception. We think about what it means to us and ascertain its connotations *i.e.* its inner meanings. This answer also means finding out what we are here for. It therefore reflects the aims and purposes of this book in so far as they contribute to the fulfilment of this answer.

What this answer is good for:
This answer is good for making us take an overall look at our lives and what we are supposed to be doing with them. If we have a clear idea of what our lives mean, this enables us to step back from everything that is happening to us and to gain more control over our lives and where they are heading. Such a clear idea can help us to make much more of life by concentrating our efforts in a few meaningful directions rather than aimlessly coasting through life without any haven in sight. Life becomes a quest to enhance the meaning that we find in it and we find joy in more aspects of life because of the additional meaning that we can put into them.

What's wrong with it:
It is wrong to think that seeking the meaning of life will automatically solve all one's personal problems. Even if its meaning were discovered, life still goes on. Inevitably, it creates problems which would not be solved by knowing its meaning. It is also wrong to have a dogmatically clear idea of what life means to the extent of eliminating flexibility and adaptability. As our lives go on, we should be prepared to rethink continually what life

means to us and change our colours according to changing circumstances. Also, we ought also to appreciate the joy of living for its own sake and not be worried all the time whether it has meaning or not. Thus, life can be meaningful without having any specific or discernible meaning at all.

Treating it as one thing:

On the face of it, there is nothing more important in life than discovering its meaning. But the meaning of life is far from being the only thing worth discovering in life. There is much more to life because we often behave spontaneously and intuitively without thought for the meaning of what we do. Dwelling too much on the meaning of life leads us to become too rational and consistent in our actions. Everything we do and think has to be related to everything else we do and think. But most of what we do is not related to any grand plan concerning life's meaning. Life is important in itself regardless of whether it can be made completely meaningful or not. We can make ourselves slaves to an overall plan to the extent of being ruled by having to do meaningful things all the time.

Treating it as one of many:

Discovering what life means for ourselves alone contributes to the enrichment of life, but it is not all there is to life. Being clear about the meaning of life gives us a set of standards by which to make choices and decisions concerning what we want to do. Though this gives unity and purpose to our lives, we need not be bound absolutely and slavishly by the dictates of these standards. We can assert our independence from such strictures by not abiding by them all the time. Freewill often consists in not doing what we think we should be doing. In that case, we can still act rationally by appealing to other answers to the problem of living.

Putting it into practice:

We put this answer into practice by examining our own lives and finding out for ourselves what we really want to do in life. For instance, we can make use of the answers mentioned in this book to choose the style of living that gives meaning and purpose to our lives. Seeking the meaning of life consists not just in thinking about life and its meaning, it also consists in doing meaningful things that enrich and make sense of one's life.

Ancillary answers:

We are here to create the meaning of life. It might be argued that we are here not only to discover the meaning of life but also to create its meaning for ourselves. The universe may lack meaning but we can bestow meaning on life which otherwise does not exist. Also, we might find a meaning in life that we, and perhaps others, have not thought of before. This might be for instance a spiritual way of looking at life that has not been thought of before. We need at least to keep our minds open to such a possibility.

The Stoical Answer:

We are here to put up with the vicissitudes of fortune

What this answer means:

This answer means that we should spend our lives coping with whatever life throws at us. It assumes that we are at the mercy of unexpected changes in fortune and that we must learn to expect these changes and make the best of them. In accepting that life is not easy, we have to prepare ourselves for all the ups and downs, the trials and tribulations, and the good and bad luck that are an unavoidable part of life. Putting up with these vicissitudes does not necessarily mean that nothing can be done about them or that they must be accepted with detached resignation. We can also put up with these vicissitudes by developing strategies for coping with them.

What this answer is good for:

This answer is good for making us stoical and hard-headed about life. It is good to put up with the vicissitudes of fortune because we can then profit from the good times while withstanding the bad times with fortitude and forbearance. It draws attention to the fact that luck and chance occurrences govern greatly how our lives pan out. It takes strength of character to forbear misfortune without collapsing under it.

What's wrong with it:

This answer is wrong in that there is more to life than merely coping with the vicissitudes of fortune. We can enjoy our lives in spite of these vicissitudes. We can take them in our stride without making a great song and dance about them. It is wrong also in that we are in charge of our lives to a considerable degree and it is too easy to blame misfortune when our own stupidity or misjudgement may really be at fault. This answer is also wrong also in making too much of self-control which can alienate us from our own feelings. We cease to share the human feelings that can prevent us from committing inhuman acts.

Treating it as one thing:

Coping with the ups and downs of life is not the only thing we have to worry about in life. If we concentrate on that answer alone then we overlook many of the benefits which life has to offer regardless of the misfortunes we may or may not suffer in life. The hardening of emotional responses is not necessarily a good thing since it can make us cruel and callous to ourselves and others. Being inured to life may make one indifferent to the misfortunes of others if that attitude is not tempered by other more sympathetic outlooks. Also, the vicissitudes of life may seen as opportunities and challenges if we do not make too much of their negative aspects.

Treating it as one of many:

We all must learn to cope with the vicissitudes of fortune, and the stoical way is possibly the best means of doing so. We accomplish nothing by allowing ourselves to become totally depressed and despondent because of circumstances which are foisted on us and are entirely beyond our control. This is more easily said than done, and actually learning to adopt the stoical frame of mind in trying circumstances is very difficult. One needs to learn to distance oneself from the emotions and impulses that are provoked by such circumstances. This is done by directing the mind to higher and better things which are suggested by other answers such as the cultural and social answers referred to below.

Putting it into practice:

We put this answer into practice by adopting a stoical attitude of mind which is hardened against misfortune and tragedy. The hardening is achieved by imposing rigid control of one's emotions and impulsive reactions to events. These events are not treated with complete indifference but are responded too in a measured and experienced manner. It is a matter of preparing the mind to respond to demanding situations and it is not a matter of looking around all the time and expecting to find trying circumstances where there may well be none.

Ancillary answers:

We here to be at the mercy of fate: This fatalistic answer is unworthy of us as free and responsible human beings. If we take this answer seriously we must give up choosing to do anything at all because everything is predestined and worked out beforehand. Such fatalism was particularly characteristic of less well developed societies in which people had far less control over their lives than nowadays. For instance, they were subject far more to plagues, famines and wars so that they may have no chance but to surrender to their fate as they could do nothing about them.

What Can We Make Of These Answers?

What we make of philosophical answers depends on the extent to which we endeavour to be philosophical persons. There is a sense in which we are all philosophers in having a philosophy of life of some kind. But the deep interest in philosophical questions demands a persistently inquisitive attitude of mind. There has to be a desire within to adopt a philosophical attitude since we are not born with it nor can we be taught to adopt it. A person's receptivity to philosophical thinking depends very much on curiosity about the things around us, worry about what lies behind things, and a willingness to think for ourselves rather than accept without thinking whatever tradition and upbringing dictates to us. These conditions do not apply to everyone and they have to come from a person's own internal development. No one can make a philosopher out of someone who lacks the pre-disposition or desire to become one.

Part Two
The Productive Approach

5
Scientific Responses

➤   *The Inquiring Answer:* **We are here to inquire into things and acquire knowledge about them.**

➤   *The Discovery Answer:* **We are here to discover things about the universe and its contents.**

➤   *The Instrumental Answer:* **We are here to make use of our knowledge for the benefit of humanity.**

What's Scientific About Them?

These responses are scientific in the wider sense of science as being the practice of acquiring knowledge in general. It is not just science in the sense of physics, chemistry, biology, zoology, the social sciences and the like. Science in the broad sense means structured knowledge which is arranged systematically. Furthering scientific knowledge demands curiosity and persistence on the part of the individual inquirer. Science is a highly productive activity which has already achieved a great deal of value for humanity. Scientific endeavour therefore demands particular attention as being a unique and productive activity fully worthy of humanity, even though it has its limitations and it can be seriously misused.

The Inquiring Answer:
We are here to inquire into things and acquire knowledge about them

What this answer means:

Inquiring into things comes naturally to us from infancy onwards. But it is not easy to carry forward into adulthood, the feelings of wonder and curiosity characteristic of childhood. History shows that cultural factors are extremely important in making it possible for individuals to harness this characteristic for the benefit of society. Thus, education is extremely important in inculcating a desire to understand and know about the things around us.

This answer appeals particularly to scientists as it refers to that attitude of mind which leads them to conduct scientific research and to theorise about the things around us. It is also called scientific because it encapsulates what science has always been about. Inquiry, questioning, curiosity, and wonder are activities which have always been particularly associated with science.

We **inquire into** things to understand them better but **enquire about** things to get specific information about them. This important distinction was noted by Fowler in his *Modern English Usage.*[*] Inquiry therefore involves a systematic study of something as compared with making an enquiry about prices in a shop or enquiring about train times, for instance. This distinction ensures that inquiry is associated with the methodical procedures of science rather than with the evanescent enquiries which we casually make in daily life.

The discovery of the scientific method that involves observation and experiment is one of the most important intellectual advances in our history. No other single discovery has transformed our lives and lifestyles more than this. For the application of scientific method has made possible all the technological advances which we have benefited from in the last three centuries or so. Though complete agreement is lacking as to what this method really consists in, there is agreement about the importance of what scientists do and agreement that science actually works. The importance of science lies in its continued progress in giving us increasingly accurate knowledge of the universe and of our place in it. Each increase in our understanding of the universe adds meaning to our lives because an item is being added to our corpus of knowledge which did not exist previously. This helps to ensure our future as an intelligent species.

What this answer is good for:

This answer is good for showing how scientific thinking is intimately connected with our normal curiosity and wonder about things. It accounts for our intelligence and why our being an intelligent species is a natural outcome of the processes of the universe. We are worthy of the name intelligent because of the vast amount of reliable scientific knowledge and understanding which we have acquired through scientific research. In that sense, science has 'saved' humanity because it justifies our proud position

* H. W. Fowler, *A Dictionary of Modern English Usage*, 2nd edition by Ernest Gowers, Oxford: OUP, 1988, p. 287: "There is a tendency, which deserves encouragement, to differentiate *enquir(e)(y)* and *inquir(e)(y)* by using *en-* as a formal word for *ask* an *in-* for an investigation, e.g. *They enquired when the Court of Inquiry was to sit.*"

as inheritors of the future of this planet. We can use our knowledge for the benefit of other life-forms, for example, by promoting biodiversity and by trying to save the planet from climate change whether it is our fault or not.

Curiosity may have killed the proverbial cat but it has been the making of the human race. Without that we would not have acquired all the scientific knowledge which has helped us to make life more comfortable and endurable than it was a few centuries ago. The curiosity of human beings gave rise to this answer and it may be traced back as far as the origin of language itself or at least to the first questions which people asked themselves and each other, prefaced by interrogative conjunctions such as Kipling's six honest serving men: what? why? where? when? who? and how? (as mentioned in his *Just So Stories* - 'The Elephant's Child' story). They are referred to on the front cover of this book. It is arguable that our brains developed by the use of such interrogations by which everything becomes questionable. In short, we develop our brains interactively by means of dualist interactions as is discussed in my book, *The Promise of Dualism: An Introduction to Dualist Theory* (2014), pages 73-95.

What's wrong with it:

It is wrong to think that we have a right to inquire into anything and everything. We have very limited faculties therefore we lack the abilities to make sense of the whole universe. We should only stick to the things that we can show that we are good at. Just as curiosity killed the cat, so our constant meddling in affairs perhaps beyond our understanding may do us more harm than good in the long run.

Also, this answer is not enough because it neglects the spiritual, moral and sociable sides of our nature. At times we must be accepting of things and not always questioning and criticising them. There is as much room in society for meek acceptance as for belligerent non-acceptance of the *status quo*. Getting the balance between these extremes helps us to ensure that our society progresses in a balanced and rational manner.

Treating it as one thing:

The success of science means that scientists are prone to make much more of its importance than is justified by the variety and range of human interests and activities. Besides, science cannot provide the answer to all the problems facing humankind. The destructive outcome of applying the scientific method and the regrettable materialism to which it leads, are often taken as excuses to condemn science out of hand. But the fact that science can be misused and can lead to mistakes being made, is no reason to condemn science itself. To be blamed are those who misuse science or who make mistakes in applying it wrongly. And science does not of itself exclude the spiritual dimension to the universe. Indeed, the new physics contains mystical elements which encourage a spiritual interpretation of the universe, as in Capra's *The Tao of Physics* for instance. Besides, only further scientific progress can save us from the consequences of flawed and inadequate technology in the past. Only with the help of improved knowledge can we correct the faults created by not knowing enough about the consequences of our actions in the past. Furthermore, it is impossible to go back to a simpler technological society without making things worse instead of better. The flaws and inadequacies of past technologies would simply reassert themselves. And in fact the very simplest technologies in the past, such as that of the hunter-gatherer culture, for instance, were just as destructive of their environment, for example, the elimination of large mammals by palæolithic hunters 10,000 years ago, and the fire-raising activities of the original inhabitants of Australia that changed the landscape to one dominated by fire resistant eucalyptus trees.

Treating it as one among many:
It appeals to the child within all of us to inquire into things and wonder about them. Many thinkers in the past have regarded science as ordered common sense. Science has its place in our culture as long as it acknowledges its limitations. Even the so-called theory of everything applies only to everything in physics and not to everything in our everyday lives. The problem is that science has been so successful over the last three centuries that its hegemony is difficult to challenge.

Putting it into practice:
This answer is most often put into practice by scientifically minded people. They are supposed to be curious and inquiring people, whether they are so in their private lives or not. Police work also requires an inquiring and inquisitive mind, as exemplified by the Sherlock Holmes and more recent detective stories. But we put this answer into practice even when we are not being scientists as such. Curiosity is not the prerogative of scientists alone. Any kind of inquiry into any area of knowledge means that we are applying this answer.

Ancillary answers:
We are here to be inquisitive inquirers. This shortens the answer by eliminating the knowledge that can be acquired by purposeful inquiry.

Clearly it is because we are by nature inquisitive inquirers that we love to extend our knowledge in that way. But we must also learn when it is imprudent to stick our noses into matters that might do us more harm than good. Children are often indiscriminately inquisitive but adults learn that often ignorance is bliss when too much knowledge causes more harm than good.

The Discovery Answer:
We are here to discover things about the universe and its contents

What this answer means:
This answer means that discovering things about the universe is a fundamental part of human nature. We are constantly discovering through the sciences of astronomy, astrophysics and cosmology that the universe is more unusual and more wonderful that we imagined. At this time, this area of knowledge is perhaps the most fruitful and interesting. We really want to know about the prospects for life elsewhere in the universe and above all we want to know whether intelligent species are living out there somewhere.

What this answer is good for:
This answer is good for the future of science since we ought never to cease our wondering and wandering to discovery new things about the universe. It is good for the human race as it helps us to understand better our place in the universe, whatever small and insignificant that place may be. But it is only as good as the scientific community which puts it into practice. Without the spectacular geniuses such as Albert Einstein, science becomes stuck in the past and cannot make the advances that it requires to keep the attention and respect of the public. This is very much the case at the moment as we await some genius to explain such puzzles as string theory, dark energy and the like.

What's wrong with it:
This answer is wrong if we think that human beings are being arrogant and presumptuous to think that they can understand the universe at all. This would be a religious attitude which is unsympathetic if not directly opposed to the scientific view. But it could also be the wrong answer if we allow scientists to believe that the scientific knowledge outclasses all other

forms of knowledge whatsoever. The answer must therefore tread the middle ground between (1) being the way forward for humanity to understand its place in the universe and (2) being not the only way for us to gain insight into our plight. The religious and spiritual view also has its place and it is not necessarily superseded in all respects by an 'omnicompetent' science. There is more on the limitations of science in my book, *Advancing Humanity: The Need To Make Our Own Future* (2016) on pages 36-50 and 228-330.

Treating it as one thing:

Physicists are inclined to think that the physical view of the universe is the only one that is really real. The common sense view that sees tables and chairs as solid objects is simply mistaken as it merely reflects the limitations of human beings. However, the common sense view is completely different from that of the physical view which really needs to be treated as one among many. For all practical purposes, even scientists live in the common sense world of solid objects. In practice, they cannot be living as if the scientific view were the only true one.

Treating it as one of many:

The scientific view cannot satisfy us unless it is treated as one of many. It gives another way of looking at reality but it is not necessarily all there is to reality. For example, much can be gained by prudent meditation and contemplation that also give us insights into our own condition. Self-knowledge requires intuitive insight and scientific knowledge can contribute to that insight but it is not the only way of gaining self-understanding. Philosophy also gives us insight by an examination of concepts and what they mean to us. This can be done without any reference to scientific knowledge.

Putting it into practice:

There is seemingly no limit to what science will discover about the universe. Recent advances in astronomy and astrophysics have ensured that new things are constantly being discovered about the universe. New technologies plus the use of computers to make precise calculations about the movements of stars and planets have yield new information about planets in distant star systems. Equally, the science of biology is revealing more and more about how life works and reproduces. All this scientific activity must raise our hopes that more secrets will be revealed about the functioning of the universe and what life is all about.

Ancillary answers:

We are here to discover the world around us. This obviously much the same as the above but it confines us to the world we live in. There is still much to discover about the depths of the ocean and about what lies in the core of the Earth. Earthquakes still need to be understood properly. We need to get to the bottom of this world just as much as we need to go beyond it and include the universe as a whole in understanding ourselves and what life is really all about.

The Instrumental Answer:
We are here to make use of our knowledge for the benefit of humanity

What this answer means:

Knowledge is not acquired simply for its own sake but also because it benefits humanity. The more we understand about our environment, our society and ourselves, the more we can bring order and purpose to our lives. We are less susceptible to the vagaries of fortune when we know what is going to happen or can calculate the probabilities of events. Knowledge in a sense belongs to all humanity since it is formulated in language that can be potentially understood by everyone using that language. The fact that it is so universally understandable means that it can be used for the benefit of everyone.

What this answer is good for:

This implies that all our knowledge acquisition is potentially beneficial to humanity. It does not exist simply for its own sake since the fact that it is knowledge means that it is potentially beneficial. In so far it is not beneficial to everyone is also knowledge that needs to be understood and used. The benefits of nuclear power are obviously countered by its misuse in the form of nuclear weapons but that is also knowledge that we are currently using to make sure that such weapons are never again used against human beings or other life-forms.

What's wrong with it:

It is wrong to think that all knowledge must be shown to be beneficial to humanity. Pure knowledge without any apparent practical benefit can still be beneficial because it is knowledge whatever its practical consequences.

Thus, this answer is wrong if it is interpreted to mean that practical benefit is required. Much valuable knowledge is acquired for its own sake and without thinking whether it will or will not benefit humanity. The idle curiosity and personal obsessions of scientists have often led to unexpected breakthroughs. Thus, Einstein, for example, was motivated in making his great insights more by sheer curiosity than by its possible benefits to humanity.

Treating it as one thing:

This answer is treated as one thing if it is implied that the only use of knowledge is that it should be beneficial to humanity. Knowledge is constantly misused and misapplied by criminals, psychopaths and terrorists. Computer knowledge is used as much for criminal purposes in hacking computers as it is for benefit of everyone. Demagogues and fanatics consider their knowledge to be ultimate and inviolable. When they use knowledge for their own benefit, it is in their view *ipso facto* of benefit to humanity as a whole. They assume that their ideas of what benefits humanity are the only possible ones so that they end up being very inhuman towards those who fail to see the obvious benefits of their ideas. In other words, this aim needs to be qualified by examining all its possible ramifications. Applying it in isolation from any other consideration may do more harm than good.

Treating it as one of many:

Knowledge should not only benefit humanity as it should also be of interest to one person at a time regardless of whether humanity will benefit from it. The pursuit of knowledge for its own sake can be beneficial even if the benefits to humanity are not immediately thought of. Though knowledge belongs to all humanity, the ends for which it is pursued are as varied as the human beings pursuing it.

Putting it into practice:

When knowledge is used to benefit humanity, it contributes to progress, well-being, health, better understanding of differences and so on. The application of increasing knowledge will only be good for us if it is used within the strict limits where it is shown to be beneficial. The disciplined use of knowledge can only come from better education in which people learn to behave in ways that benefit humanity and not just themselves or their peer group. Only by thinking critically about what we are doing can we be sure that we are really benefiting humanity by what we do.

Ancillary answers:

We are here to use our knowledge responsibly and thoughtfully. This answer perhaps corrects the tendencies of the above answer that result in the misuse of knowledge. What we think intuitively to be beneficial to humanity may in fact not be so. It is therefore necessary to be responsible and thoughtful in our use of knowledge and not be misled by the apparent obviousness or reality of our conclusions about the world and how to set it to rights. What is really the case is discovered by constantly reviewing the views critically and not by accepting one set of facts as being ultimate truths. Moreover, it is not enough to rely on the wisdom of crowds which is sometimes correct when common sense is involved but it is the madness of masses when passions and feelings are inflamed. But even common sense can be misleading otherwise we would still believe that the Earth is flat and the sun goes round the Earth. There has to be a healthy interplay between the views of the public and those of individuals. For reason and good sense must prevail over emotional commitment of any kind.

6
Ecological Responses

> *The Gaia Answer:* We are here to be in harmony with the Earth.
> *The Saving Answer:* We are here to save the planet from the consequences of human abuse.
> *The Caretaker Answer:* We are here to husband the planet on behalf of other life-forms

What's Ecological About Them?

Ecology is defined as the study of the relationships of living organisms to their environment. Therefore, these answers are ecological because they concern the ecology of the planet, that is to say, the complex interrelationships between life-forms and the environment which they have created for themselves on this planet. These answers go further than the mere study of these interrelationships as they have acquired a political and even a religious dimension. They voice people's concerns about what the human race is doing to their environment. What is meant by the Earth or the planet is not just the water, air, rocks and minerals that make up the physical world we call the Earth. It includes all the life-forms and life processes which envelope the physical Earth. Thus, it is more accurate to say that we are referring to the biosphere which forms part of the geosphere of the Earth. The biosphere in turn constitutes such a unified and interconnected system that it has been personified as 'Gaia'. It is arguable that this ecological trend goes too far in the latter respect, as is argued below.

The Gaia Answer:
We are here to be in harmony with the Earth

What this answer means:

This answer means that we are all intimately entwined with all the processes going on around the planet Earth. We get into harmony with the Earth by respecting the contents and processes which make the Earth work as a unified biosphere. This answer implies that the human race is out of harmony with Earth at the moment and that efforts should be made to harmonise our relationships with these contents and processes that make the planet a suitable place for life to thrive and survive. It refers not so much to the planet Earth as physical entity but more to the biosphere of life-forms that have developed scum-like upon the surface of the planet. It is called the Gaia answer because the biosphere of the Earth is being treated as an organism which has a life of its own over and above the lives of all the life-forms which are dependent upon the harmonious continuance of the processes making up the biosphere. This view therefore reflects the fashionable 'New Age' pre-occupation with the Earth and the adverse effects which we are having on the planet. There is also a meditational sense to this answer. We can think ourselves into harmony with the Earth by means of meditation and contemplation. This is not however the ecological meaning of this answer that is being discussed here.

What this answer is good for:
This answer is good for emphasising the inescapable fact that we are a part of everything that happens on this planet. It is good to be aware of our need to be in harmony with everything happening on the planet, especially as a consequence of what we are doing to the planet. We need to be in harmony because we are painfully aware of the extent to which we are out of step with Mother Nature. Global warming is now shown to be the consequence of our activities. Species of animals and plants are continually being made extinct because of what we are doing to the planet. We have been pursuing our own interests blindly and thoughtlessly for far too long. We now realise that being in harmony with the planet is in our own interests.

What's wrong with it:
This answer is wrong only in so far as we have as much right to exploit the planet as any other life form on it. We have been produced by the same evolutionary processes as other life forms. The big difference between ourselves and other life-forms is that we have the knowledge and expertise which enables us to be aware of the effect that our activities are having on the biosphere. They have the bliss of ignorance whereas we have the guilt of knowledge. However, it is natural for us to exploit the planet for our own ends as it is for any other species to exploit the planet. Also, it is wrong to be certain that our paramount need is to be in harmony with the Earth. The damage that we do to the planet and the harm that we have done to countless living species is nothing compared with the catastrophes to which the biosphere has been subjected in the past. Various natural causes such as asteroids, volcanoes, ice ages and so on have wiped out far a greater percentage of life-forms on Earth than we can possibly do. Yet the

biosphere has always bounced back. Indeed, we wouldn't be here in the shape that we are if the dinosaurs, for instance, had not been wiped out sixty million years ago.

Treating it as one thing:

When this answer is applied monistically it devalues the activities of human beings. Our activities are viewed entirely from the point of view of their effects on the planet. The fact is overlooked that progress is continually being made towards becoming more harmonious with the planet. There is such a lack of patience with this slow progress that advocates of this answer want us to regress to a simpler state of society. They want us all to be miserable for the sake of the whole planet.

Treating it as one among many:

That we should live in harmony with the planet, is something that few of us would quarrel with as a principle. But when it threatens to depreciate our private lives, we are liable to forget it too readily. This can happen when we are expected to curb our own extravagant activities to save money and save the planet. If we all become as ascetic and self-denying as these ecological answers demand then the collapse of national economies will result because people are no longer spending their money and keeping the wheels of industry turning. This is why the politico-economic answers must be taken into account. Since we are already a part of everything happening on the planet, our affairs must form an equal part of any harmony to be aimed for. If we beggar ourselves as a species we are liable to be even more destructive of the planet in our desperate attempts to eke a living out of the planet. Thus, the future lies seeking a balance between our own endeavours and the needs of the planet to avoid global warming and all the other harm we are currently doing.

Putting it into practice:

This answer is put into practice when we support all the political efforts to ensure that we live more in harmony with the biosphere. But it should be done in a methodical and scientific way rather than by stirring up extreme emotions in the Greenpeace way. We have to use our heads rather than our hearts in achieving harmony.   Otherwise we will lose control of our position on this planet and become, once again, subject to natural, evolutionary factors instead of being the worthy masters of the planet which we can become provided we work hard at this task. This way of putting this answer into practice requires collective action on the part of us all. There are also things that we can do as individuals to make our contribution towards achieving harmony with the planet. For instance, we can put this answer into practice by consuming only environment-friendly products, eliminating wasteful practices, binning rubbish, taking part in recycling schemes and so on.

Ancillary answers:

We are here to serve or worship Gaia. The above view can be taken to the extremes of making a god, or rather goddess, of Gaia. What we are trying to get into harmony with is personified to the extent of making a superior being of it. Just because it is bigger than us doesn't make it superior. The fact that we know enough about it to make a science of ecology means that it is anything but god-like. It is a science for us to put into practice not a religion to be foisted on us willy nilly. It is the epitome of earthiness rather than godliness. We can hardly be more down-to-earth in our thinking than when we are concerned about our effects on the environment. Gaia is best thought of as an object of knowledge not of adoration.

The Saving Answer:
We are here to save the planet from the consequences of human abuse

What this answer means:

This answer refers to the mess that we are making to the planet and the threat to other life-forms because of our activities. Saving the planet implies that we are meant to do something about the consequences of our abuse of the planet. That abuse includes the pollution that causes global warming, the pillage of natural resources, the threat to animal and plant species, the plight of underdeveloped nations whose resources are exploited by developed nations. It presumably means that we can save the planet by organising ourselves to cope effectively with the consequences of our abuse of the environment. Above all, it implies that we have to take seriously what we are doing to the biosphere instead of behaving as if everything will sort itself out in the natural course of things.

What this answer is good for:

This answer is good for confronting us with the flaws and deficiencies of our socio-economic system which often takes little account of the consequences of its activities on the planet as a whole. It is good that we should make a clear aim of cleaning up the planet and relieving it of all our ill-doings. We can't just do whatever we like with the planet merely because there appears to be nothing to stop us. The fact that we can do something does not mean that we should do it. We don't expect individuals to commit murder merely because they can do so. Similarly, the human race as a whole needs to impose limitations on its activities for purely moral reasons. We should do it because it feels right and makes us feel better in doing it.

What's wrong with it:

This answer is wrong because clearing up the messes of the past is not the only concern of human beings. Individuals have the right to put their own livelihoods before any other concern. People living at subsistence level are much more concerned with their survival than with the effects of their activities on the planet. Making ecological matters paramount means preventing people in underdeveloped countries from becoming self-sufficient simply because their activities may be harming the biosphere. In the Amazon basin of South America, for instance, it is difficult to prevent individuals from making an honest living as farmers. It is easy for us to take the high moral stance because we in the more advanced countries can see things from a higher perspective. The only viable solution is perhaps to help bring underdeveloped countries up to the same level of development so that they can afford to be more environmentally conscious.

Treating it as one thing:

If this is made the chief end of human activity then we will start to abuse ourselves and threaten our own future. The good things that are accomplished by our civilisation would be sacrificed for the sake of life-forms that have no awareness of what is being done for them and can show no gratitude for our self-sacrifices. The fanatical application of this answer would simply eliminate human beings from the picture altogether. If we are taken out of the picture then the biosphere simply reverts to being subject to blind chance. Since we are here and can possibly develop the technology to save the biosphere from future natural disasters, it follows that we have the opportunity to benefit the biosphere instead of threatening it as in the past. Those who go to the extreme of wrecking the economy to start afresh seem not to understand how the world economy functions. It reacts to criticisms of that kind so that something is done about them, otherwise blind chance takes over.

Treating it as one among many:

Most people would probably agree that one of the things we have to do as species is to save the planet from our misdeeds. The problem is how this laudable aim is to be fitted in with all our other legitimate aims in life. It seems to be a matter of priorities. There are priorities such as reducing population size, eliminating inefficient, polluting industrial activity, encouraging waste recycling and so on. But such priorities can only be achieved apparently by getting the rest of the human race up to the same standard of living as is enjoyed in advanced nations. In that way, family sizes are reduced and industry activity becomes more efficient and less wasteful and polluting.

Putting it into practice:

Putting this answer into practice therefore involves adopting the measures mentioned in respect of the previous *Gaia answer*. It is important for the harmony of the planet that we have a plan for combating human abuse rather than destroying everything that the human race stands for. Now that we are here and have made our own mark on the planet, it would do more harm than good for us to regress to Stone Age living since that would do nothing to remedy the damage that we have already done to the planet. We have to use new technology to rectify the faults caused by old technology. We must go forward to better things and not regress to much worse things.

Ancillary answers:

We are here to save the planet. Simplifying the answer in this way only broadens our responsibility. It makes our task more difficult if not impossible, as it includes saving the planet from asteroids, solar flares and other threats over which we have little or no control. Also, it is not clear why we should have to save the planet. Until we admit our responsibility for the mess that it is in we have no particular responsibility for its future. This implies the need for the *Caretaker Answer* now to be dealt with.

The Caretaker Answer:
We are here to husband the planet on behalf of other life-forms

What this answer means:

This answer means that we are responsible for the wellbeing of other life-forms on this planet because we have the science and technology to take on that responsibility. Husbanding the planet means researching into our impact on it, planning to reduce that impact and to make the most of its resources without threatening the wellbeing of other life-forms. It is called the Caretaker Answer because we are expected to take care of the planet and assume responsibility for everything that happens on it. It might also be called the 'stewardship' answer although the word 'stewardship' is more specific than 'caretaker' in stressing that we are serving the planet in a menial position. We are employed to serve because we take on that employment rather than have servitude thrust upon us. We are taking care of the planet because there is no one else around who seems to be doing anything about it. We can no longer pretend that God has anything to do with such matters even if such an entity did exist. We are beholden to no one but ourselves in this caretaker function. Therefore, we had better perform the duties of this position to the best of our abilities, if only because there seems to be nothing else for us to do.

What this answer is good for:

This answer is good because it brings out what it is true and worthwhile about the ecological movement. Unlike the other two answers above, it does not involve deifying 'Gaia' or making much more of the biosphere than we make of ourselves and our own concerns. It is good for making clear our responsibilities without also implying that the biosphere is more important than we are. The biosphere is not more important than we are because we are as much a part and product of it as any other life-form on Earth. It may be said to be more important than any life-form which is subject to it and incapable of comprehending it or of consciously doing anything to it. But we are capable of making sense not only of the biosphere but also of our role in respect of it. We can therefore take care of it as we, as individuals, take care of each other. The biosphere is our fellow companion which is our equal and not our superior in any absolute way.

What's wrong with it:

This answer is wrong because it assumes a degree of arrogance on our part that we have the right to husband the planet. But that right doesn't come from nowhere. We need to justify it by reasoned argument and with convincing evidence. We should establish why we have such a right and whether we are really worthy to take on this responsibility. It is wrong to think that we know with any certainty what it really means to husband the planet. Our knowledge and understanding of how the biosphere functions is strictly limited. Unless and until we have the technology required to manipulate the climate, maintain the ocean currents and so forth, we cannot be said to be in charge of the biosphere or have any real control over it. We have enough difficulty trying to protect endangered species from depredators of our species: ivory hunters, whalers etc. How can we protect living species in general when the endangered ones are in danger from ourselves?

Treating it as one thing:

If we organise ourselves to do nothing else but look after the planet, then we would be neglecting many of our own interests. These interests remain paramount while we must exploit the planet and its resources to live a decent life. No doubt we are slowly working towards a position where our presence on the planet is transparent and unthreatening to the biosphere. But until we can ensure our own survival and future prosperity as a species, we have to make that our priority. When that is assured then we perhaps can turn our total attention to husbanding the planet.

Treating it as one among many:

This is another example of an answer at which we have to work hard to incorporate it with other answers that may be dearer to our hearts. For husbanding the planet is more a political matter which is of less concern to most people than the problems of day-to-day living. It becomes more of a problem for an increasing number of people when their personal problems are less immediate and all-consuming. They have time and patience to consider wider issues and concern themselves about higher matters than simply feeding themselves or finding somewhere comfortable to live.

Putting it into practice:

We put this answer into practice by being much clearer than we are at this time about what our responsibilities are with regard to the biosphere. Having clarified these responsibilities we then have to work out in great detail just what we must do to carry out these responsibilities. It is perhaps necessary to make a Great Plan about how the human race must in the future disengage itself from its effects on the environment by developing the technologies which would enable it to be self-sufficient of everything that is happening on the planet. This possibly means burying our cities underground, living in the oceans, populating the Moon and so on.

Ancillary answers:

We are here to be caretakers of the planet. This answer simplifies the above answer but also suggests that we are meant to lord over other life-forms according to our own whims and selfish ends. It begs the question why we should take on that responsibility and it makes us seem arrogant and overbearing. Why should we lord over other species? What makes us think we are so important? Perhaps the answer is that we do it because we can, and no other species is in a position to do so.

What Can We Make Of These Answers?

We can clearly make as little or as much of these answers according to what we feel about our relationship to the biosphere. Most people give very little thought to the state of the planet, let alone worry about what they should do about it. Creating the conditions where people begin to feel more strongly about such matters depends, as has been argued, on their having the time and opportunity to lift their thoughts to such higher concerns. Ecological concerns are a luxury which only people in advanced nations can afford to enjoy. Eliminating industry and making us poorer would only make it impossible for us to care for the planet at all. We would continue to wreak havoc on the planet as we have ever done in history, only we would do so out of desperation and not because we want to. Advanced civilisation at least gives us the opportunity to do something about the state of the biosphere however little that may prove to be.

We have two globalisations to choose from. (1) The globalisation of the biosphere being achieved by increasing knowledge of the connections between livings things, the climate and the physical environment generally. (2) The globalisation of the human race as it organises itself increasingly in economic, political and cultural terms. As these globalisations conflict with each other, the difficulty lies in the consequences of carrying out both of them together. There has to be an accommodation and reconciliation between them. Hence the importance of matching up the *Ecological Answers* with the *Politico-Economic* ones which are now to be dealt with.

7
Politico-Economic Responses

> *The Political Answer:* **We are here to be political animals.**
> *The Economic Answer:* **We are here to contribute to the economic prosperity of the human race.**
> *The Lucrative Answer:* **We are here to make money.**

What's Politico-Economic About Them?

These answers are called politico-economic because they are about the value of political and economic activity to the human race. They refer to the role of politics and economics in understanding the nature and structure of the complex society in which we live. Both these areas of thought give us a measure of control over what is happening in society. They do so by correcting imbalances, bottlenecks, misunderstandings, and everything concerned with making society work for all of us. They are interactive sciences rather than predictive sciences. They are better at reacting to correct faults rather at predicting them. Politics and economics are inextricably linked in modern society because the control of the economy has great political consequences. Politicians may have lost control of certain aspects of monetary policy such as setting the bank rate, but they still have control over taxes, government spending, the level of industrial activity and so on. The sphere of politics goes beyond that of economics though economics is wholly within the sphere of politics.

The Political Answer:
We are here to be political animals

What this answer means:

This answer means that being political is an essential part of what it is to be a human being. We can be either politically minded or politically active and we can both at the same time. In being politically minded, we take an interest in what happens to society and to the human race as a whole without necessarily doing anything about it. In being politically active, we take action to put forward our views and see them carrying into action. To that end we join or create political parties, write books, articles and letters on political matters, and so on. This answer implies that every adult is politically involved in society whether they are aware of it or not and whether they like it or not. For politics affects us all whether or not we pay any attention to it. Indeed, we may be said to differ from other animals in that we are politically oriented and are prone to take an interest in political affairs.

What this answer is good for:

This answer is good for reminding us that our actions have political consequences whether we are aware of that fact or not. Virtually everything we do has some political implications and connotations of some sort. Politically speaking, we begin with behaving politely or impolitely since our behaviour has effects on other people and that sets the political climate of our neighbourhood. Thus, in the widest sense of the word 'political' we may be said to be political animals. Moreover it is good for us to think of ourselves as political animals because it emphasises our sociability and our need to relate meaningfully with each other in a social context.

What's wrong with it:

This answer is wrong in that it makes too much of politics. We are more than just political animals and many of the other reasons of living demonstrate that fact. Besides, what Aristotle really wrote was that human beings are city dwelling animals.* He didn't really mean 'political' in our sense of the word. In modern parlance, he meant more 'sociable' rather than 'political' animals, since everyone in the city was expected to be polite and civilised (both these words coming respectively from the Greek and Latin for 'city'). Nowadays, we don't normally regard all our sociable actions as being political since the word refers primarily to the concerns of politicians, political parties, pundits and political journalists.

* πολιτικὸν ζῷον, *politikon zōon* - the Greek *politikon* means that which is associated with the *polis* or city – *Ethics* I, vii, 1097b; *Politics* I, ii, 1253a.

Treating it as one thing:

Politics is taken up by many people who consider it to be the only activity worthy of them. It becomes their whole lives to the exclusion of anything else. But the idea that politics has an importance overriding anything else, applies to simpler societies whose problems need strong leaders to overcome them. Nowadays, politics has become so professionalised and marginalised by all the multifarious activities of a complex society that it matters much less than it used to. Politicians are no longer expected to be great leaders but only competent professionals who respond to the needs of their constituents and to the pressures of mass media concerns. Indeed, leading politicians are now more like celebrities who have little executive power except a free access to the media to voice opinions which are already known before they even speak.

Treating it as one among many:

Our role as political animals can never be totally eclipsed while there are still problems of a political nature to be sorted out. The ecological answers discussed above are an example of outstanding problems which will only be satisfactorily sorted out by political means. Thus, politics is important as long as it takes account of the other answers which need political thought and action if they are to be implemented effectively. Politics is a means to ends outside the political activity required to implement these ends.

Putting it into practice:

We put this answer into practice, as has been already mentioned, when we join a political party, take an interest in political matters, discuss them with other people, vote at elections, voice our political opinions by contacting politicians, or write books, articles and letters to newspapers. But all that does not necessarily make us political animals as such. Perhaps we all need to be at least politically minded people but only politically active in so far as limited aims and purposes are concerned. This means that piecemeal social engineering is to be preferred to utopian social engineering. Planning should be confined to tackling specific problems instead of forming an overall plan which purports to be all inclusive.

Ancillary answers:

We are here because we are politically inclined in some way. This answer goes beyond the above to make out that we are perhaps genetically inclined to be political animals. But we are also equally inclined by our natures to be solitary as well as sociable beings. It is normal for us to seek a balance between being wholly exposed to the public on the one hand and living entirely to ourselves on the other hand. Perhaps we make too much of politicians and celebrities by putting them in the limelight all the time. The solution may come when we all voice our opinions online by voting on matters that used to be the province of parliament. Politicians would then appeal directly to the public to support the viewpoints which they work out professionally and present to us from a more expert point of view than the rest of us.

The Economic Answer:
We are here to contribute to the economic prosperity of the human race

What this answer means:

This answer means that by participating in the economy as consumers, producers, employers, employees, capitalists or whatever, we are contributing, as if by an invisible hand, to economic prosperity. That prosperity depends on our being enterprising and business-like in our behaviour. It is not just our national economy which is at stake nowadays. It is the prosperity of all humankind. All modern economies are so intricately interconnected through globalisation that no one nation stands alone in generating prosperity. Because of the ever-increasing interchange of goods and services between nations, the prosperity of all nations is intimately dependent on the prosperity of other trading nations. Furthermore, all our economies are dominated by multinational organisations which no longer have clear national allegiances. We thus contribute as much to the world economy as to our national economy by our efforts in the workplace. Ultimately, this answer means promoting the work ethic because it implicitly values the importance of work. Unless the majority of people pull their weight by working as hard and as efficiently as possible, the continued prosperity of humankind is under threat.

What this answer is good for:

This answer is good for making us think about how our prosperity depends on the activities of the whole human race. It is an antidote to narrow nationalism which wants to restrict trade with other nations in the hope of protecting indigenous industry. Such a restriction of world trade threatens the prosperity of the world economy because that prosperity depends on nations specialising in those economic sectors in which it excels. For example, if Japan shows an ability to produce cars better than any other country then it is to the benefit of us all that the Japanese specialise in doing that. In that way we all benefit from the efficiency of other nations. It is also good to have an informed view of how the world economy works and how the livelihoods of us all depend on its continued prosperity. Even underdeveloped nations have no prospect of ever reaching the living standards of advanced nations unless that world economy continues to develop and prosper. Smashing up that economy will only increase the suffering and misery of all humanity and not just those fortunate enough to live in advanced nations.

What's wrong with it:

This is wrong because human activity is not just confined to ensuring economic prosperity. Indeed, economic prosperity itself depends on people's philosophy or attitudes of mind. Unless we have a philosophy of spending money to make a good life for ourselves there can be no economic growth or prosperity. Unless we have an optimistic philosophy about the future and increasing knowledge about the universe, the economy will suffer because our future is under threat. There are therefore aspects of human activity which are more important than the pursuit of economic prosperity because without these aspects there can be no prosperity. These include research activities from which new technologies can emerge. Academic research is important as it stimulates human thought. Entertainment is important because it diverts the mind and refreshes people so that they can return to more arduous pursuits with renewed vigour.

Treating it as one thing:

This answer panders to the single-minded aims of tycoons and captains of industry. It justifies their narrow-minded concentration on money making for its own sake. When our contributions to economic prosperity become the sole end of our lives, we lose the capacity to see ourselves as unique and valuable individuals. We become cogs in the economic machinery. Our value lies only in our work and in what we achieve or fail to achieve in the work environment. Economic prosperity for its own sake can also soften people and increase immorality and bad behaviour generally.

Treating it as one among many:

Nevertheless economic prosperity is extremely important to the human race. Without it, nothing else worth doing can be accomplished. Economic prosperity enables projects to be carried out which an unprosperous economy cannot afford to support. This answer therefore accompanies many of the other answers as it is not only compatible with them but also contributes to and benefits from the fulfilment of these other answers to our being here. Such economic prosperity can only be ephemeral if it does not accompany a vision of where we going as a species and what we are aiming to do with our lives. If the vision is not brought down-to-earth and put into practice in a realistic way, it is no more than a passing dream.

Putting it into practice:

We put this answer into practice by being enterprising and business-like people. Whatever we do that is valued by other people should earn us money and thus prove us to be enterprising and economically viable people. But this is not always the case because the economy is governed by public opinion and fashion on the one hand and the interests of big business and multinational companies on the other hand. Our particular contributions to society may not be recognised as worthwhile because of these polarising interests. We may have to fight to make our mark on the marketplace if we regard our contributions as undervalued.

Ancillary answers:

We are here to be businessmen, accountants, lawyers etc. Ancillary to the above are all the professions related to business, trade and commercial activity. It is all too easy for professionals to be immersed in their own profession and underrate all other human activities. Their professions become ends in themselves and they cannot see beyond them. The object of this work is show that this is a narrow minded way of thinking and that everyone, no matter what their profession or mode of living, should look beyond their own answers to see the merit and worth of other answers even though they may have no wish to incorporate them into their respective lifestyles.

We are here to be economists. Those interested in using economic theory to understand the nature of prosperity and how to sustain it, may consider economics to be the answer as far as they are concerned. But the success of any economy does not just depend on the accurate implementation of economic theory. It depends on a combination of factors including the implementation of that theory. It depends also on the spirit and enterprise of the people involved in the economy, on the availability of new technology and inventions by which the economy may be invigorated, and so on. Without the latter, the economy cannot function and prosper, no matter what the economists do or how accurate their theories are concerning how complex economies function.

The Lucrative Answer:
We are here to make money

What this answer means:

This answer means that making money is the most important aspect of our lives. We need money to live therefore money is indispensible and the most important aspect of our lives. We make money by being employed, by going into business, by trading or exchanging goods, by being of service to others, and so on. Generally, we make money by making ourselves useful to others in a social or economic context. Money is the means by which modern society enables us to get out of it what we want both as individuals and as contributors to the economy.

What this answer is good for:
This answer is good because money may be taken for granted in advanced nations where no one need lack money for the necessities of life. Our self respect depends greatly on our being able to make enough money to keep ourselves. Money is good for us and those who scorn it often are inept or incapable of making money for themselves. Their attitude to money is one of sour grapes. They wish to spoil other people's enjoyment of it because they are not able or willing to enjoy it themselves.

What's wrong with it:
This answer is wrong because money is not everything.   The lust of making money can bring out the worst in people. They are liable to take short cuts in their eagerness to make money. Greed is not good if it leads to lawbreaking or the destruction of people's lives in a bloody minded scramble of the almighty dollar.   What is overlooked are conceptions of honour and high-mindedness. These ensure that money is not sought for its own end but for the same of better causes which do us honour and demonstrate the extent of our high-mindedness. A plutocratic society is one that values wealth and money before anything else, whereas a meritocratic society values people doing their best for the best reasons. Money is only a means used by a complex social structure to place a value on different kinds of activity. When it becomes an end in itself, everything is valued in terms of money instead of for its own sake. Monetary value subjugated to public opinion and fashionable trends. It is as mindless as the masses who misuse it for ephemeral and self-serving purposes.

Treating it as one thing:
People make one thing out of making money when they have nothing else on their minds but accumulating more and more of it. As with any other human activity, making money can become an end in itself. Those who put money before anything else are liable to become criminals, gangsters, extortionists, misers, and so on. They take short cuts to lay their hands on more money than they are legally entitled to. Even the banks have lately lost their erstwhile reputation for integrity and reliability in their self-centred scramble for profit based on other people's credit. Whole nations can be corrupted by the pursuit of money for its own sake. Such nations

may have no future because they have no ideals to live up except the base and corrupting one of moneymaking. Even more tragic is the constant accumulation of credit to purchase more and more goods and services, thus creating a bubble of non-existent money that must sooner or later burst with predictable consequences.

Treating it as one among many:

Money is a part of life in every complex society. It has been re-invented in every human society which has reached a certain level of complexity in its economic activity. We all need to make money to live well but that does not mean that it should come before all considerations whatsoever. This answer should therefore accompany many other answers which involve doing and accomplishing worthwhile things. Earning money is supposed to be the reward for doing something of value to society and our fellow human beings. The satisfaction should come from the end product and not the means of achieving the transaction. In other words, one should feel pleasure because of the service performed or the value of the goods to the customer rather than because of the money gained as a result of the transaction.

Putting it into practice:

This answer is put into practice when we become wage earners, successful business persons, or simply good at selling things, making ourselves useful to others, and so on. But we need not value our lives entirely by our money making ability. What is done with money is more important than the getting of it. Money is a social implement by which value can be put on goods and services. Money belongs to no individual since it is a function of the society that confers value on money. Thus, those with great wealth have an obligation to society to use that money as much for the benefit of others as for themselves. The wealth does not belong to them so much as it is entrusted in their possession. They are being trusted to use their judgment and discretion to use that money for the best possible purposes. That this philanthropic role of money is easily forgotten nowadays goes without saying.

Ancillary answers:

We are here to be bankers, moneylenders, stockbrokers, etc. Ancillary to the above answer are all the professions and middlemen linked with the handling of money who have the object of making money out of money. They contribute to the world economy by facilitating the flow of money and by easing bottlenecks which prevent money from being as freely available as it needs to be to ensure prosperity. They have a responsibility to society which recently many of them have forgotten completely in their eagerness to enrich themselves without thought of the consequences.

What Can We Make Of These Answers?

We have to make something of these answers if we are to live in the real world and have reasonably satisfying lives. If we make nothing at all of them, then we are presumably living poverty stricken lives with little future or prospects. These answers help us to participate in society in such a way that we are contributing in a concrete ways to the politico-economic wellbeing of society. But these answers are to no avail if the world economy fails to continue its economic development and to give opportunities to participate in it to an increasing number of its participants.

8
Cultural Responses

➢   *The Competitive Answer:* **We are here to differentiate ourselves as individuals from other people**
➢   *The Talent Answer:* **We are here to develop our talents for the benefit of society.**
➢   *The Aesthetic Answer:* **We are here to be creative artists and fill the universe with beauty and significance.**

What's Cultural About Them?

Our culture is the product of the civilised society into which we are born. Culture is "the total of the inherited ideas, beliefs, values, and knowledge, which constitute the shared bases of social action" (Collins Dictionary). It includes everything wholesome and meaningful which we enjoy about living in this society now - the films, television, theatre, sport, books, hobbies and so forth.

The above cultural answers refer to those organised activities that help us to develop our talents and abilities for the benefit of society as a whole. These answers are favoured by a great many people because we must function within a cultural context whether we like it or not. They help us to make sense of our living in a changing society that is becoming ever more complex and difficult to understand. Even if we cannot quite understand what modern society is all about, we can nevertheless make something of our own lives by referring to such answers. In that way we can learn to use the changing complexity of society for our own benefit because we are clearer in our own minds what we want to get out of it. We can expand our mindset to accommodate more conveniently the complex circumstances with which it must cope to make the most of our circumstances. Thus, education is extremely important for the future of our culture in that it inculcates the skills and knowledge that we all require to make the most of the complex society in which we live.

When we pay attention to and act on these cultural answers we invariably do things which add value to culture as well as to our own lives. We add value by doing things our own way to make a unique contribution that makes sense of our lives and leaves society better off. Thus, the whole point of having a culture is so that we can contribute to it and get something back from it. The cultural answers reflect the most important ways by which we can do this.

The Competitive Answer:
We are here to differentiate ourselves as individuals from other people

What this answer means:

We differentiate ourselves from other people by behaving in ways that are consistent with our unique individuality. When we are not differentiating ourselves from others then we are mimicking their behaviour, saying what others want to hear and not expressing our own opinions, following fashionable trends mindlessly, and so on. It is part of being a useful human being that we should cultivate aspects of our personality which are unique to ourselves and owe nothing to the influence and example of other people. This competitive answer is sociable at least in the sense that other people are involved. The competitive person needs other people to compete with. What is more, the purpose of competing with them is to differentiate oneself as an individual by doing things differently. Thus, the person who puts particular emphasis on this answer is keen to distinguish him or herself for strictly social purposes *e.g.* to make their name, to make money, become rich or whatever. This is not necessarily a good thing in itself but it is perhaps something that we should all aspire to do as part of our life-plan.

What this answer is good for:

This answer is good for stressing the importance of individuality and self-assertion. Our differences from other people can be seen as being good and valuable in themselves. It is an essential part of our growing up to take our rightful place in society that we should have a firm grasp of what we are and what we can do. If we are relying on others to give us a lead in this then we will lack inner conviction as to what we can or cannot do as unique individuals.

What's wrong with it:

It is wrong to be different all the time. Though we are all potentially unique individuals, we lose the opportunity to demonstrate the value of our uniqueness if we accentuate our differences too much. We alienate ourselves from other people by being too different. There is a basic raft of similarities which we all possess by virtue of being human beings. We have to exploit these similarities to make the most of our differences. We have to accentuate our similarities with other people just as much as our differences. If we all make too much of our differences then we will fall out with each other and live for ourselves alone. Shaw's play, *Back to Methuselah*, demonstrates what can happen when people cultivate their own individuality to the exclusion of their interaction with other people. They become hapless sages who blunder around aimlessly until they are killed off by some accident such as lightning or a tree falling on them.

Treating it as one thing:

This answer can be taken to eccentric and anti-social extremes when an individual makes too much of their differences from other people. A person who differentiates themselves too much from others is probably prone to deep seated feelings of inferiority and inadequacy. They are compensating for these feelings by showing how different they are from other people. This answer was brought to the fore in the middle of the 19th century with the works of Darwin and Herbert Spencer. Evolutionary theory makes too much of the struggle of the individual for survival and not enough of the co-operative behaviour of living beings. It was also presaged in the work of Hobbes who saw us as being competitive individuals who are perpetually are war with each other.

Treating it as one among many:

There are obvious limits to the extent to which we can profitably differentiate ourselves as individuals. But this answer is taken as part of a balanced life plan then we can establish by trial and error experience just how we can and should differentiate ourselves from others. We can mitigate the implications of differentiation by ensuring that it conforms to the demands of other answers such as the other cultural ones mentioned below. These give purpose and discipline to the application of this answer by helping us to become creative artists and by aspiring to do our best and benefit others, and so forth.

Putting it into practice:

We put this answer into practice by finding ways of differentiating ourselves, at least to our own satisfaction. In our quest for self-identity, we need to find that level and type of differentiation which suits us as individuals. In becoming self-confident and productive individuals we learn to be content with differentiating ourselves only up to a point and no more. The difficulties of putting it into practice include the attachments and obligations which we have in life. Thus, this differentiation process is always a balancing act in which our social commitments temper our will and ability to make ourselves different from others.

Ancillary answers:

We are here to be different. This is just a truncated version of the answer above. It serves to accentuate the act of being different. It therefore adds to the faults of the above answer by focusing on the word different. The above answer uses the verb 'differentiate' and qualifies it with reference to the relationship of ourselves to other people. This emphasises the social nature of being different. There is no use being different unless there are other people around from which we can be different. If we are all equally different then we might have difficulty finding things in common by which to interact socially with other people.

We are here to be distinguished people. This brings to mind the Warhol dictum that in the future everyone will be famous for fifteen minutes. This obviously democratises the idea of fame to an absurd and impractical degree. In reality, not everyone wants to be famous for even one minute, and at the other extreme some people are never satisfied no matter how famous and distinguished they become. The prospect of fame and distinction thus brings out the élitism which is inherent in human nature. Some people want and deserve to be distinguished, others neither want it nor deserve it but get it nevertheless. Between these two extremes, there is every variety of desire for fame, or the lack of it.

The Talent Answer:
We are here to develop our talents for the benefit of society

What this answer means:

This answer follows on from the previous one and focuses on the importance of everyone's talents from the point of view of society. A talent is an innate ability, aptitude or faculty which makes the possessor special and unique. In theory, everyone has talents which are special and unique to themselves. The answer assumes that everyone has talents that can be developed and will be of benefit to society. This assumption may be confirmed or denied by empirical evidence provided that it is generally agreed what a talent is and how society benefits from such talents. The problem is that no such general agreement exists as everyone can have their own idea of what talents are and how they benefit society. Nevertheless most people would probably agree that the talent answer is a good one despite all the uncertainty surrounding it. The fact is the whole rationale of our society depends on people displaying their talents and using them to benefit society one way or another.

What this answer is good for:

In so far as people agree with the import of this answer, it is good for the future progress of society as it depends on talented people bringing into being new and different things that enrich our lives. Talented people can fill our lives with hope and enthusiasm and can justify the existence and prolongation of the human race. It is also good for the well-being and self-respect of individuals that they develop their talents and are recognised for the contribution of these talents to society as a whole.

What's wrong with it:

What's wrong with this answer is that not everyone is talented or believes themselves to be talented in any way. They are liable to be jealous of those who are talented. Untalented people are also essential to the running of society. Talented people are notoriously unsuited to a hum-drum, everyday existence and may not be reliable or dependable. Also, we can make too much of people's talents or the lack of them. It is perhaps better for people to be themselves regardless of whether they are said to be talented or not. We can overtax people by expecting them to have talents when they may in fact be content to be mediocre non-achievers. They too have their place in society and their role is not to be disparaged merely because they are conceived to be untalented people.

Treating it as one thing:

Being a talented person is not everything there is to life. We need to be well-rounded persons who can function as normal people regardless of any exceptional talents that we might or might not possess. Also, it is a matter of opinion as to what is or is not a talent. In a sense, everyone is talented if they are able to do anything for themselves. Thus, this answer is trivial if the meaning of talent is extended without limit. It is also restrictive and élitist if it refers only to those talented in the narrow sense of being famous and celebrated for their talents.

Treating it as one among many:

Talented people contribute to society but so do ordinary, untalented people. The importance of the latter has to be recognised by ensuring that being regarded as talented or not talented is not necessarily the be-all and end-all of existence. For people with limited abilities, the performance of the simplest tasks can be a triumph which they are proud to herald. These tasks constitute their talents and it may serve no useful purpose to belittle them by comparing them with more talented people. However, from the point of view of improving and furthering society, it is necessary to promote people of outstanding talents that can contribute to welfare and progress of society.

Putting it into practice:

We put this answer into practice by cultivating people's talents wherever it is found. We have to recognise talent in others as well as in ourselves. It is in the interests of society that everyone should cultivate their talents and make the most of them, however limited and commonplace these talents may be. The education system in particular needs to be developed in the direction of exploiting people's talents. As well as inculcating the skills and facts needed to function efficiently in society, the education system should also bring forth everyone's talents such as they are.

Ancillary answers:

We are here because we are all talented in some way. This answer narrows the field down to our being unique human beings who have hidden talents that might be developed out of that uniqueness. If we are all different from each other in identifiable ways then there must be a way in developing these differences so that they are productive in some way. In that our talents might be identified and developed for the benefit of society. Unfortunately, our education system is a long way from making such identifications as each person would have to be examined more minutely than the current system allows. Perhaps the enhanced use of computers will eventually make such differentiation possible.

The Aesthetic Answer:
We are here to be creative artists and fill the universe with beauty and significance

What this answer means:

A creative artist is commonly regarded as someone who can create something which is recognised as a contribution to art and culture. An artist may be a painter, sculptor, poet, composer, writer, etc. Our society is inevitably élitist in its view of such creativity as many are called but few are chosen in so far as they are regarded as contributing to human culture and civilisation. Not every one is sufficiently talented as an artist to make a worthwhile contribution of the highest quality. Such contributions are supposed to satisfy the high standards laid down by art critics and aficionados, not to mention art-loving members of the public. Yet the tastes of the public may be questionable when apparently trivial things are regarded as being 'art'.

Moreover, as a species, we are naturally creative and inventive creatures and this answer exploits this facet of human nature. The populist view is that everyone is potentially creative, inventive and ingenious in their own way. Everyone has something potentially unique and original to contribute to culture, if only they have the training, education plus the will and tenacity to tap the well of originality waiting within them to be discovered and brought out. Both the élitist and populist views are substantially correct within their own context and there is surely room for both of them in our civilisation.

What this answer is good for:

This answer is good because it helps us to respect and value both our own creative abilities and those of others. It is good for encouraging everyone to find out what their creative abilities are and to develop them accordingly. It appeals directly to the individual to make the most of their talents and abilities regardless of the apparent social or cultural value of their creative contributions. It is good for society that a never-ending flow of talented people comes forward to enrich our lives and show us just how creative and original the human being can be.

What's wrong with it:

This answer is wrong in that being a creative artist is a very sophisticated, culture-bound activity. It is not possible for anyone to be a creative artist unless they are endowed with talents and have been trained, educated and conditioned to use skills and abilities which they can only acquire within a cultural context. A person can be totally uncreative and inartistic and yet still be a perfectly viable and useful human being. Indeed, unless some people are not creative and artistic is not possible to be clear what being a creative artist is. There are also artistic and cultural standards to be maintained and these standards are threatened by the possibility that everyone might consider their creative contribution to be the equal of anyone else's. Such standards depend on the encouragement of truly talented and able individuals and on the discouragement of those whose talents and abilities are judged by public opinion, critics or pundits to be inferior and their works to be worthless or degrading.

Also, it is not necessarily the case that creative artists should fill the universe with beauty and significance. Some forms of art may be judged ugly, scary or insignificant, and yet their perpetrators may be considered creative artists. One person's work of art is often another person's lump of crap. *Chacun à son goût* – each to his or her own tastes.

Treating it as one thing:
This answer goes beyond the first two answers in that our creativity is being emphasised. It is not enough to exist or to make a difference. It is also necessary to create something of beauty and significance to leave behind us. Our aesthetic inclinations are very deep rooted and may be traced back at least to Neanderthal peoples who, according to archaeological evidence, arranged flowers in the graves of their dead relatives and created ornaments.

This answer was taken to monistic extremes by philosophers such as Schopenhauer, Nietzsche and G.E. Moore in his *Principia Ethica*. However, Schopenhauer only refers to this answer as being the highest culmination of the will in its creative mode. He does not make more of this answer than for instance the Christian and Eastern asceticism which he seems to commend in other parts of his book, *The World as Will and Representation*. Nietzsche takes the idea of creativity to its logical conclusion in his philosophy by arguing for the paramount importance of the artist's life and contributions to society. Moore, on the other hand, argues for the importance of the aesthetic approach as a way of life, a view that was taken up enthusiastically by the Bloomsbury Set, which included such luminaries as Virginia Woolf, John Maynard Keynes and Lytton Strachey.

Treating it as one among many:
This is certainly one of the most important answers to the problem of what we are here to do with our lives. We are all creative to some degree and the future of humanity depends on creativity renewing the spirit and enterprise of our civilisation. Novel ways of doing things and thinking about them are continually required to invigorate our culture and renew people's enthusiasm for life and living. There is doubtless a creative artist in us all but whether we can in fact create something of real and lasting valuable to culture and community depends on having real and talent. One can only find out whether one possesses such talent by trying different things.

Putting it into practice:
We put this answer into practice by finding out by trial and error those activities which we not only enjoy doing but also bring out a creative flair

within us. We ask a great deal of ourselves in putting this answer into practice. We must think in much more culture-bound terms to establish what is or is not a creative addition to culture. We thereby become to a greater or lesser extent responsible as individuals for the cultural heritage of humanity. At the same time, the more diverse and complex that our society becomes, the more opportunities arise for those whose talents and abilities may have been overlooked or undervalued in the past.

Ancillary answers:
We are here to make music, paint, perform the arts etc. Every method and technique by which we express our creativity and artfulness provides an answer of its own that will suit someone whose talents are brought out and appreciated by the public. However, the kind of art that is of interest to the public depends very much on vagaries of fashion. It takes a very brave and persistent artist to create a fashion for their particular form of artistic expression.

We are here to be geniuses. This answer is by no means incompatible with the aesthetic answer but follows on from it. However, it expects too much of us. Being a genius means standing out from other people and being one of few who have accomplished something which so-called 'ordinary' people only dream of doing. Thus, we don't all expect or want to be geniuses. And not everyone wants their prescribed 'fifteen minutes' of fame. Besides, even those who believe that they have the talent and ability to be 'geniuses' in their chosen field, are not always acknowledged as such, no matter what they do to accomplish that aim. What is or is not a genius is itself highly contentious and bound up with fashion and pure chance.

What Can We Make Of These Answers?
This depends greatly on the culture we live in and the environment in which we are brought up. A great deal of moral luck is involved. We have to lucky in our genes, parents, upbringing, historical timing and so on. Without such luck many people would have done nothing with their lives. Equally many people have accomplished astonishing things in spite of adverse circumstances. Much therefore depends on ourselves and the strength of will within us. Provided we can maintain the inner strength to keep on going in face of indifference, discouragement, and criticism, we can achieve a great deal. This is the message of Samuel Smiles in his book, *Self-Help*, and other self-improving works.

9
Sociable Responses

> *The Co-operative Answer:* We are here to be nice to each other.
> *The 'Golden Rule' Answer:* We are here to do to others as we would want them to do to us.
> *The Moral Answer:* We are here to do our best and to make life better for ourselves and others.

What's Sociable About Them?

These answers are sociable in that they concern our relationships with other people in a social context. Being a sociable person means being someone who can make friends and interact successfully with other people in the workplace and elsewhere. Each of these answers emphasises the importance of being socially interactive. They concern how we behave to other people and how we cultivate relationships to make the most of our lives. Networking is the in-vogue term which describes what sociability usually means, that is to say, the establishment of networks of friends, acquaintances, colleagues, contacts etc. A sociable person is generally thought to be a better adjusted, more mature and well rounded than an unsociable person; such are the benefits of interacting with other people.

These answers involve us personally since they give expression to our personalities. When they involve us personally and become part of our personal make-up then they automatically make us sociable and gregarious. The cultural answers of the last chapter lead to conduct which can contribute impersonally to cultural development. But the solipsistic ones in the next chapter may have no cultural bearing whatsoever even though they involve us in social relationships. There is therefore a spectrum running from the most impersonal to the most personal which begins with the cultural answers, through the sociable to the solipsistic answers.

The Co-operative Answer:
We are here to be nice to each other

What this answer means:

Being nice generally means being pleasant and accommodating with people. A nice person does not antagonise people but treats everyone well and with the great respect. But what it means to be nice to each other is often a matter more of opinion than of fact. We are only nice in so far as we influence someone's opinion about ourselves so that they interpret our conduct and the things we say as being acceptably nice and sweet. Thus, people's judgments may be very superficial and uninformed concerning what is or is not nice behaviour and who is or is not a nice person. Also, problems arise because everyone knows how to act nice and because it is difficult to judge whether people really are nice or are simply acting nice for their own unspoken interests and motivations.

This is the answer which we give when we think intuitively about our sociable nature. As we are by nature sociable and amiable animals it is natural for us to like being nice to each other. Children in particular tend to assume the niceness of everyone they meet and they have to be warned against trusting all strangers. However, we are also exploitive animals who are out to use people for our own ends and this is where the niceness of people often breaks down.

What this answer is good for:

This answer is good for accentuating the niceness that is in us all whether it comes naturally to us to be nice or not. Being nice to each other also enables us to co-operate more effectively. It is very difficult to get on with people who are deliberately being nasty and unpleasant all the time. Unless a person is nice as a rule then they are scarcely able to function as a viable human being. It is good not only for human relationships but also for civilisation that we try hard to be nice to each other even though it may require effort and willpower on our part.

What's wrong with it:

It is wrong to think that being nice to people is necessarily a good thing. Niceness is a behavioural trait which may be used by scoundrels, hypocrites, gangsters and criminals to exploit and undermine other people. The fact that a person behaves or acts in the nice way does not mean that they are really nice people. Thus, to encourage everyone to be nothing but nice may just create a society full of smarmy hypocrites. Also, being nice to each other all the time can be very tiresome and artificial when our feelings tell us that we cannot stand the people we are interacting with.

Treating it as one thing:

Thus if we rely on this answer alone as a solution to the problem as why we are here, then we automatically divide the human race into nice and not nice people, according to how we intuitively react to them at the personal and emotional level. Excessively nice people often provoke an equal and opposite reaction by annoying others into being nasty and by allowing them to take advantage of their niceness and exploit or undermine them in some way.

Why we can't be nice to each other all the time:

We may well ask why can't everyone be nice to each other all the time? Why is it considered impracticable idealism to expect this to be the case? Some of reasons are as follows:

- People are often nasty to each other because of the inherent differences between them. These differences perhaps make universal niceness impossible. People will never be agreeable enough to each other to be considered nice for any length of time. They will take exception at each others' lifestyles, opinions, appearance, clothing and so on. Familiarity may breed contempt. People become bored with each other and fall out as a result. Also, they will not feel like being nice to people who are too different from them.

- Some people are incapable of being nice to everyone, either because of their nature or because of their experiences of life. They may be constitutionally incapable of relating to people in a sociable manner. Perhaps they have been hurt by others in the past and so they are nasty out of self-defence. Others are nasty because they like to prey upon nice people whom they regard as soft, inferior, contemptible or whatever. Some people take pleasure in not being nice. Misanthropic people have always been around and they serve to remind us that the human race is ever full of flaws and obnoxious traits.

- We tend to like or dislike people and, as a result, give preference to some people over others. This makes niceness suspect because it is based on this instinctive liking or disliking which may be founded on inclination and not be borne out by any evidence or indeed the truth of the matter. If we dislike a person, we may simply consider them not to be nice.

- We take offence at what people say to us and therefore regard them as not nice people. Strangers constantly misunderstand each other, especially when they are joking, or think they are. The Duke of Edinburgh has always been notorious for his jokes that the media deliberately and unfairly misinterpret as being offensive. A single incident can lead people to jump to conclusions concerning the whole character of the person. For instance, a misplaced word taken the wrong way can engender negative thoughts and feelings which lead a person to become nasty to the perpetrator.

- We constantly disappoint each other in our expectations of each other's conduct. We are always showing ourselves to be weak, unreliable, inefficient, annoying, offensive, ridiculing, disrespectful or to have other intolerable shortcomings that make people want to be nasty and inconsiderate towards us. Young people are often impatient with the foibles of old people so the one may regard the other as not being a nice person.

- Besides, some religions in the past have placed a particular emphasis on niceness. For example, Christianity itself began as a great experiment in bringing niceness in the world: 'love thy neighbour as thyself' and so on. It failed spectacularly because Christians have never had much love towards those who differ slightly from them, even those who are as committed Christians as themselves. Their neighbourliness was not extended to heretics and non-Christians. Buddhists are also typically laid-back and nice but even they have their limits and have lately been burning themselves and feuding and fighting with Moslems.

Treating it as one among many:

Though it pays to be nice to people and to have people being nice to us, the niceness is best confined to an identifiable and limited context. We are not usually surprised or apprehensive when a shop assistant is nice to us. We expect to be treated nicely in that situation. Thus, it is helpful to be clear in our minds just why a person is being nice to us - because it is their job, because they genuinely like us, and so on.

Putting it into practice:

We are nice in practice by virtue of the behaviour which others construe to be 'nice'. Hopefully by learning to behave ourselves as nice people, we become nice people inside ourselves as well as by virtue of our outward appearances. But we need reasons within ourselves for being and acting nice all the time. For we usually put this answer into practice because we benefit in some way from being nice to people. When we don't benefit personally then we have no reason to be nice all the time. In order to eliminate nastiness in our social interaction it is necessary for us to be mindful of any possible or imaginable benefits that we might gain by being nice to people whom our feelings repel or our judgments despise.

Ancillary answers:

We are here to love each other. This answer was very much in vogue in the late sixties as it was popularised by pop stars and those of a 'hippie' mentality. 'All you need is love' proved not to be enough of an answer even for those who thought it was at the time. But many of them were already into drugs to make their aimless lives more bearable, so that 'all you need are drugs' might be a more accurate assessment of their lifestyles. The Roman Empire was founded on the principle that everyone was supposed to love the Emperor. This often meant either dying for him or being killed for not loving him enough. The principle ended up in the worship of the Emperor as a god. In short, love for its own sake must lead to an irrational worship of the object of love. It therefore seems safer, though more boring, to respect each other rather than love each other.

We are here to please each other. This answer is stronger than the co-operative one and it is virtually ancillary to the self-immolating answer below. It goes further down the line towards ingratiating ourselves towards other people. It is indeed the answer of those of a particularly slavish mentality.

We are here to be cruel to one another. This is ancillary to the co-operative answer in that we must sometimes be cruel to be kind. It is also a useful antidote to the wetness of that answer. It is natural for us to be cruel towards people whose behaviour lays themselves open to it. This gives rise to the bullying of vulnerable people who are preyed upon by people whose inadequacies lead them to vent their nastiness on other people.

The 'Golden Rule' Answer:
We are here to do to others as we would want them to do to us

What this answer means:

This is one of the most universal ethical rules in the world. It is a reciprocal answer which implies that the way we behave towards other people is reciprocated by similar behaviour towards us. It means doing nothing to other people except what we would expect other people to do to us. This answer is called the 'Golden Rule' because of its obviousness and its ubiquity. A similar sentiment has arisen independently in religions and ethical systems throughout the world. It is found for example in Christianity, Confucianism, and Buddhism.

What this answer is good for:

This answer is good because it is an antidote to selfishness and disregard for the well-being and interests of other people. It makes us think of others in the same terms that we think of ourselves. We learn to think about the effects of our actions on others in respect of how we would react to these same actions if we were to experience them ourselves. We thus sympathise with other people because we see something of ourselves in them. It also gives us the power to see ourselves as others see us. This view was developed by Adam Smith in his *Theory of Moral Sentiments*, Part Three, Chapter One.

What's wrong with it:

It is wrong to think that we will benefit from thinking about others all the time. If you only do what other people expect of you then you will loose all individuality and become a pawn in other people's hands. It is also deficient in that there is a limit to the extent to which we can and should be sympathetic towards other people. If they do not deserve our sympathy then it is questionable whether we should to them only what we want them to do to us. Perhaps they require correction, punishment or treatment which we would not expect or deserve from them. It comes into conflict with the idea that we should differentiate ourselves from other people. If we sympathise with other people then we identify with them and overlook our differences from them.

Treating it as one thing:

Kant used the golden rule as the basis of his ethical system. He treated it as a categorical imperative that we should make a law of doing only what we would expect others to do in the same circumstances. We should only behave in such a way that we can universalise that behaviour and expect to see others behave in the same way. However, this has authoritarian consequences in that everyone is expected to behave in the same way without exception. This is altogether too much of a good thing. It makes for a very boring society if no one is allowed to behave differently from anyone else.

This answer also brings altruism to the fore. Because we are sociable animals we are not entirely self-regarding. We are also altruistic when we think about others and of putting ourselves in their position. We have the power to see ourselves as others see us though we have to work hard at perfecting and maintaining this power. Seeing the benefits that our unselfish acts can bring may be pleasurable in itself.

Treating it as one among many:

We need not always do to others what we want them to do to us because we are all different and need to be treated differently. You might say things to someone which you would not want them to say to you. You can hurt people's feelings by doing things to them that you would not mind at all if they were to do these things to you. It is therefore necessary to absorb the truth of the Golden Rule in order to go beyond it. It is applied as a general rule but not without exception. One does to others what will be for their own good as much as because one expects the same treatment from them.

Putting It Into Practice:

We put this answer into practice by using our judgment to ensure that what we do to others does not in fact differ from what we would have them do to us. And we put it into practice by making a policy of sympathising with other people whenever they appear deserving of our sympathy. In that case, we must assume that they are deserving of our sympathy until they clearly show themselves not to be so deserving. Thus, in practice, this answer is strictly limited by the sympathy or lack of sympathy which we have towards others.

Ancillary answers:

We are here to trust one another. This answer follows from the reciprocity of the Golden Rule answer in so far as it implies that we do things for each other. A large measure of trust is necessary for human relationships. Indeed, it is indispensible for business relationships. 'My word is my bond' is not for nothing the time honoured motto of the London Stock Exchange. Our lives are dependent everyday on the trustworthiness of all the goods and services that we enjoy. However, it is the case that, as Robert Burns put it: "Mankind are unco weak and little to be trusted" ('Epistle to a Young Friend'). But it is our very weaknesses that bring us together and make us need each other. As individuals we can be as pathetic as new born infants but as a unified purposeful species we are undoubtedly the most formidable species on this planet in so far as we can make or break it. Can we therefore trust ourselves to make the most responsible use of our strength?

We are here to enter into reciprocal relationships with each other. This answer involves the golden rule since a reciprocal relationship means a giving and taking on a broadly equal basis. In getting what we want and giving what others want, we have to put ourselves in other people's shoes and make exchanges on a rational and equitable basis.

The Moral Answer:
We are here to do our best and to make life better for ourselves and others

What this answer means:

Doing our best means applying our judgment to our own actions and motivations to ensure that we make the best choices in the things we do. This can make life better for all of us because doing our best means aiming for consequences which will benefit ourselves and others to the highest possible degree. Doing our best makes life better because what is judged and showed to be best leads to better things. This is of course easier said than done. The road to hell is paved with the best of intentions, as the proverb goes. The same applies to making life better for others. We make a hell for others and ourselves by trying to make people better according to our own view of what is better. For all we know, we make things worse for others by doing the most beneficent things we can think of. Thus, doing our best does not necessarily mean that we will make life better for ourselves or others. But the object of doing our best is that of making life better in that way.

What this answer is good for:

This answer is good because it stresses the role of morality in making us look to the best within ourselves and others. It is good for encouraging us to use our evaluative and judgmental capabilities to establish what is for the best. Trying to do our best gives us legitimate goals in life. Even if we do not attain these goals, we may achieve much of value in attempting to reach them. For instance, in trying to be the best in one's profession, one may achieve a level of satisfaction without achieving everything that one sets out to achieve. This answer therefore is essential for self-improvement and for making a better person of ourselves.

What's wrong with it:

This answer is wrong because there is no reliable way of establishing that we are meant to do our best. Nor can we establish what is best except by referring to our own predetermined ideas concerning what is best. Also, our best may often prove to be not good enough. As a result, we lose confidence in our ability to do anything if we are demonstrably deficient in some respects. Comparing ourselves with the best which other people can do is also demoralising and discouraging. This answer favours an élitist, aristocratic kind of society in which the many are looked down upon by the few who are clearly shown to be better than them because of their social position, wealth or whatever.

Treating it as one thing:
In so far as we have developed the ability to judge between good and bad we know how to make things better. We can do so because we have acquired skill, abilities, knowledge and understanding to make things better. But whether things really are better as a result is a question which can always be raised. If it is a fact that we can make things better, then we have a responsibility to do so if only because there is nothing else for us to do. Thus, the argument is ultimately circular since we have no choice.

Treating it as one among many:
From time to time, we all need a rest from being good and from forever striving to do our best. Indeed, it is only by doing things badly that we learn do things better. It is wise not to expect too much of ourselves. Skills and habits that are improved little by little over a long period of time are liable to last. (They are of greater benefit in the long run than the bad habits such as drug-taking that we pick up easily because they are popular activities.) The élitist, aristocratic nature of this answer means that it has to be tempered by more democratic answers which recognise the value of each human being regardless of whether they are better or worse than other people. Thus, the *Aesthetic Answer* below can help the individual realise their creative ability regardless of their cultural or élitist value. The *Universal Answers* and the *Sociable Answers* can also offset the élitist and aristocratic bias of this answer.

Putting it into practice:
We put this answer into practice by using our judgment and discernment to limit and channel our activities towards those which we judge to be for the best. When we have in mind nothing but the best and do not settle for anything less then we are putting this answer into practice. When we are certain that things will be better for ourselves and others as a result of our most considered actions then we will have done our best to put this answer into practice.

The implementation of this answer may be limited by the state of development of society that prevents us from achieving the best we can hope for. Thus, the further development of the social structure should also provide more and more opportunities for individuals of all ranges of ability to better themselves.

Ancillary answers:

We are here to attain perfection. Doing our best and making things better are steps towards perfection and the next step is to make an aim out of perfection itself. Perhaps we should all aspire to perfect ourselves. Perhaps we are really doing that from day to day, as in the classic film, *Groundhog Day*. It is sometimes as if we are repeating the same day trying to make it as perfect as possible but invariably failing, sometimes in the details, sometimes catastrophically, depending on how things pan out.

What Can We Make Of These Answers?

The sociable answers cannot be accomplished through intuition and good feeling. Our feelings are too pushed towards the other extreme of unsociability when we react emotionally to the words and actions of other people. Our feelings are such that they vacillate too easily between liking and disliking people, especially when we know little or nothing about them. Someone who is perceived to be nice person immediately becomes a nasty one as soon as they say or do something that annoys us, meets with our disapproval or whatever. It is only by building up an objective stance in relation to the words and deeds of others that we are able to curb our feelings of hatred and enmity towards those who are different from us in objectionable ways. 'Sticks and stones may break my bones but words will never hurt me' – this is an easy mantra to chant but actually putting it into practice is much more difficult than saying it. The ultimate goal of this 'nice' answer is that of promoting human harmony by helping people to achieve a more detached perspective concerning our fellow human beings.

That we should all be nice to each other and not hate or quarrel with each other is an obvious ideal that has never yet been accomplished, as is argued above in the *Co-operative Answer*. The continuity of our civilisation depends on our not letting mutual animosities grow into a chaos of hatred and dissension in place of the relatively ordered social system that presently exists in the developed world.

A moral system is perhaps unavoidable as a set of basic guidelines by which to live one's life within limitations that take account of one's relationship to the human race as a whole. What is avoidable is a rigid and unfeeling moral code which is imposed on individuals from external sources such as the state, religious organisations or other hierarchical organisations. For what is proposed is a moral system which provides guidelines by which individuals may relate themselves to the needs and aims of the human race as a whole, without any external agency telling them how to behave and what they have do.

The spectre of a moral system conjures up images of a Victorian morality which at the present time is considered by many to be undesirable and intolerable. But the archetypal Victorian morality works by the application of external pressures on the individual. A more humanistic morality can only work by appealing to the individual's internal moral sense. A person who lacks this moral sense will be immune to all moral considerations except those that appeal to naked self interest. It is therefore important that the individual learns to think through things in a moral way as opposed to a purely self-interest way. This is only possible by encouraging humanistic thinking which encourages the individual to expand their thinking towards universal as opposed to selfish concerns.

Part Three
The Counter-Productive
Approach

10
Solipsistic Answers

> *The Self-Indulgent Answer:* **We are here to please ourselves.**
> *The Hedonistic Answer:* **We are here to enjoy ourselves.**
> *The Self-Centred Answer:* **We are here to seek answers for ourselves in our own way.**

What's Solipsistic About Them?

Solipsism is the view that the self is the only thing which can be known to exist. The philosophical doctrine of solipsism is distinct from the psychological attitude of being solipsistic. People who are solipsistic will interpret everything in relation to themselves because they are so focused on their own concerns that they behave as if everything revolves around them and nothing else is of any consequence. But no one can be totally solipsistic without being excessively autistic and self-regarding. A completely autistic person is incapable of appreciating other people's thoughts and feelings. However, solipsistic person is concerned principally with their own affairs and can learn to think differently by appreciating the importance of other people's concerns and interest.

Thus, in this context, a solipsistic answer tends towards solipsism but cannot be totally solipsistic to the point of being autistic which may be an irremediably psychological condition. The above answers are solipsistic in so far as they are self-oriented and betray an excessive inclination towards selfishness. The term 'solipsistic' is deliberately pejorative because selfishness is usually not to be encouraged in anyone. This is not just because we are a social species; it is also because we benefit as individuals by thinking of others besides ourselves, as the *Sociable* and *Self-Sacrificing Answers* indicate. In making use of solipsistic answers, the individual is looking themselves alone. Thus, these answers are solipsistic in that the existence of other people is ignored, overlooked or undervalued in their self-interested pursuits. Their own feelings and interests are paramount, and other people's feelings and interests are at best marginal and at worst irrelevant to their own.

The Self-Indulgent Answer:
We are here to please ourselves

What this answer means:

Pleasing ourselves agrees with us either intellectually or emotionally. We are pleased when we have decided that this is what we want to do or because it makes us feel better within ourselves to do it. It means looking to our own thoughts and feelings first and foremost. It thus means putting aside, overlooking or not caring about the expressed needs or unspoken feelings of others. On the face of it, this is a self-indulgent, self-serving and self-centred approach to life in which one wants to please oneself regardless of what other people feel or think. It is usually a pejorative comment if a person says 'Please yourself' when they really want you to do something you don't want to do.

What this answer is good for:

This answer is good in that we need to please ourselves to develop our inner strength and well-being. It is good for reinforcing our rights as individuals that we should be ourselves and do as we please within the law. Also, by pleasing ourselves we can learn how to please others. When we are pleased about ourselves we are more inclined to feel good about other people. Indeed, the fact that others are being pleased can only be understood if one knows what it is to be pleased oneself. To be appreciate others we have also to appreciate ourselves and we can only appreciate ourselves by being self-indulgent and self-regarding to some degree.

What's wrong with it:

This is wrong because we are not really here to please ourselves at all. If we were then we would be totally hedonistic creatures which never did anything but stimulate the pleasure zones of our brains. We only like to think that we are here to please ourselves when in fact we can only get away with pleasing ourselves some of the time. Most of the time, we barred by circumstances, other people, physical limitations etc from doing what we please. In fact, we spend most of lives pleasing others because it is easier than antagonising people all the time.

Treating it as one thing:

It is the height of self-indulgence to do nothing but to please oneself. It is characteristic of the spoilt child that he or she is not taught to do anything else but please him or herself. But it is more reprehensible when an adult goes on to spend his or her whole life pleasing themselves. Pleasing oneself is all about freedom. The totally free person is the only one who can really please himself in the things he wants or does not want to do. But for finite creatures such as ourselves, total freedom is illusory. We end up tying ourselves down one way or another.

Treating it as one among many:

It is only human to please oneself, but it is also human to feel guilty or shameful about doing so. It pleases us also to please other people at times, and even our pets and plants. Ideally, we should only please ourselves when we are pleasing others. But this leads inevitably to some form of servitude. We can also learn to be pleased with the things that we are necessary for us to do, although that is easier said than done.

Putting it into practice:

This answer is easily put into practice since most of us in the wealthier areas of the world are brought up to please ourselves. Our parents usually make sure that we learn what pleases us and what does not please us. In fact, we are spoilt rotten unless we also learn that we can't get everything we desire and want. It is through caring for others that our desire to please ourselves is lessened. Thus, the sociable and cultural answers are useful in conjunction with this answer.

Ancillary answers:

We are here to be pleased about everything. Only in a perfect, unattainable world can we expect to be pleased about everything in life. We would have no incentive to do anything but contemplate our navels if that were the case. It is because we are hardly ever pleased about anything for very long that we have developed and, on the whole, prospered as a species on this planet. Long may that continue.

We are here to be pleased by others. This is the master/servant kind of answer. Dominant people are liable to make servants out of their nearest and dearest. They expect to be served hand and foot. It appears that enormously fat persons may come into that category. They turn themselves into feeding machines by being fed by all too willing relatives who fear the consequences of not catering for their insatiable appetites.

The Hedonistic Answer:
We are here to enjoy ourselves

What this answer means:

Enjoying ourselves *per se* means stimulating our inner feelings so that we feel good and have a buzz of well-being inside ourselves. Being here to enjoy ourselves means that we avoid doing things that distress us, depress us, annoy us, bore us, or give us pain and discomfort. Yet it might be argued that any of the latter can be found enjoyable when we are presumably in a self-abnegating or sado-masochistic state of mind. But these states of mind are unusual and perhaps abnormal, so that we need not make too much of them in any definition of what enjoying ourselves consists in.

We should always try to enjoy ourselves but the real question is whether we are really enjoying ourselves or merely fooling ourselves into believing that we are. We therefore have to be clear about what it is that we are enjoying ourselves at, and about the extremes to which we are prepared to go to obtain enjoyment. We must ask not whether it is right that we should enjoy ourselves but what we are meant to enjoy ourselves for and how far we should go in that enjoyment. If it is not the case that we are here to do nothing but enjoying ourselves all the time we must ask why this is so.

What this answer is good for:

This answer is good because we need to enjoy ourselves in life for the sake of our health and well being. Enjoyment is necessary to sustain our interest and commitment to whatever we are doing. Enjoying oneself makes particular sense when we spend a significant amount of our time not enjoying ourselves. In this way the contrast ensures that our enjoyment is all the better and more intense because it compares strikingly with the hardship that has gone before.

What's wrong with it:

It is wrong to try and enjoy yourself all the time if only because we are achieving nothing. The effort of doing something useful may be unpleasant but the end-result may give us pleasure and make the discomfort worthwhile. Some pain, suffering and unpleasantness are good for the human soul. Enjoying oneself all the time not only leads to a vegetative, mindless state of mind, it is also boring. It is often wrong to enjoy oneself in circumstances where others are not enjoying themselves. Enjoyment is very often to be had in company with others, and it is rude, insensitive, and unsociable to have fun in a group where one or more are not having fun. It is still more objectionable to have enjoyment at others expense.

Treating it as one thing:

This selfish answer brings our self-interest to the fore in a way that the former answer fails to do. For it means not just pleasing ourselves but confining ourselves to things that give us enjoyment. It is the ultimate answer which we can all appreciate but not all of us want to live a life which is nothing but pleasure-seeking. We may adopt such a life-style but it does not necessarily suit us all in the situations in which we find ourselves. A hedonistic life-style might worthy of the most ideal society but it is at best only fleetingly found in any human society today. It is an ideal state of affairs that we should do nothing but enjoy ourselves. It is simply a hard fact of life that not all of us are able to enjoy ourselves all the time. Not only that, we are also liable to take upon ourselves challenges which may not be entirely enjoyable in themselves. Achieving them, however, may of course give us enjoyment.

Treating it as one among many:

Enjoying ourselves, like pleasing ourselves, is about exercising one's freedom to do what one chooses. We all need to enjoy ourselves from time to time. The question is whether it is really necessary to be enjoying ourselves all the time. After all, enjoyment can be had from doing pretty taxing and challenging things, such as climbing mountains, crossing deserts and icy wastes and so on. Apparently there is no limit to the dangerous things that human beings can find enjoyment in doing.

Putting it into practice:

This answer is also very easily put into practice since enjoying ourselves comes naturally to us as long as we have sufficient health and wealth to be able to do so. Learning how to cope with not enjoying ourselves all the time is a more important lesson for us to learn. There is also a time and a place for having fun and this has also to be learnt. The most important lesson to learn is the fact that we can experience great enjoyment from doing difficult, demanding and challenging things. Enjoying ourselves does simply mean having sex, drugs, drink, a good laugh and other immediate forms of pleasure. After all, we can enjoy ourselves simply by making ourselves useful to others. Indeed, we can learn to find pleasure in doing things that we have hitherto found boring.

Ancillary answers:

We here to eat, drink and be merry. This merely makes more specific the modes of enjoyment that are favoured by any individual who sees this answer as being appropriate for them. We should all enjoy eating, drinking and being merry but these kinds of activity are often an evasion of the problems of life. They are a palliative rather than a panacea. Carousing and partying allows people to hide away from the business of living.

We are here to have fun. This answer is particularly favoured by those of an adolescent mentality. Such individuals think that no one can be enjoying themselves unless they are also having fun. Even more adolescent behaviour consists in thinking that nothing is worth doing unless one is having a laugh. Indeed, the most cruel and anti-social acts are often justified by the simplistic attitude that they are good for a laugh.

We are here to have sex. This answer came into increasing vogue during the twentieth century because of the work of Freud and other sexologists. This is a biological answer which is on a par with saying that we are here to excrete, urinate, scratch ourselves or whatever. The answer is not necessarily true of human beings, as abstinence from sexual activity has long been advocated by wise men throughout the ages. People today make too much of sex just as the Victorians allegedly made too little of it. Much more important than having sex with people are the cultivation of affectionate, caring relationships which have nothing to do with sex. As sexual activity is basically an animal function, it does not become us as human beings to make too much of it. Its lasting importance to us lies only in the fact that we need it to reproduce the species. Otherwise, it is an ephemeral and meaningless act which tells us nothing about what we are as human beings. In developing our personalities and in becoming socially useful individuals, we benefit from relegating sexual activity to a relatively trivial and unimportant part of our lives. Even when we disregard the need for social restraints, our personal health and well-being may depend on rational control of sexual behaviour. What constitutes rational control is something we all must establish by personal experience.

The Self-Centred Answer:
We are here to seek answers for ourselves in our own way

What this answer means:

This answer is self-centred in that we look to ourselves alone in seeking answers. We consult our own resources and assume that others have nothing to tell us that we cannot find out for ourselves. We don't expect any help in finding the answers which we pose to ourselves. We feel justified in this because no one can find the answers in quite the same way that we can ourselves. We learn things more thoroughly when we find out things for ourselves. Thus, the self-centredness comes from making this answer an end to all our activities whatsoever. All education and learning depend on our finding out things for ourselves in our own way but only because of the ends to which such education and learning can be put. Such activities are a means to an end and not an end in themselves. But this answer implies that seeking answers in that way is an end in itself. It is therefore self-centred because the end is selfish and not outward-looking. Unself-centred education and learning is a building up of inner resources to cope more effectively with the world in which we live. But increasing self-centredness occurs when education and learning continues for its own sake and not because of any outward use that can be made of it. Thus, a great deal of research in our universities comes into this bracket of fostering self-centredness rather than producing well-rounded individuals eager to go out into the world and make their mark on it.

What this answer is good for:

This answer is good because it encourages people to rely on their own judgment rather than on the judgment of others to give them the answers all the time. It is good for making people more independent and mature in their outlook. Our will and our judgment require to be developed by working out our problems in our own way. We come to terms with our own abilities and resources by getting ourselves together, preferably in solitude. One way of doing this is to consider as many options and choices as possible and formulate a life plan based on these.

What's wrong with it:

This answer is wrong because other people's answers may do us very well. We may in fact do ourselves more harm than good by seeking our own answers when the answers that are already available may suit us better. We may also waste years of our lives and cause ourselves untold suffering by obstinately looking for own answers when the already available ones are the ones we really need. It is wrong to think that others have nothing to teach us when only blind arrogance and immaturity prevents us from seeing the faults and deficiencies within ourselves which others can help us to remedy and alleviate. We must at some point trust other people's judgments and recognise that our own judgments are never the last word on the matter.

Treating it as one thing:

Taken to its logical conclusion this answer is the ultimate in solipsism. The idea that we are entirely on our own in working things out for ourselves is about as self-centred as one can get. Our idea of the mad scientist plotting to destroy the world is an extreme example of someone who wants to do everything their own way. One's own answers are as likely to be wrong or to mislead us as be correct and wholesome. It is only by comparing our answers with those of others that we can be sure that we are on the right track.

Treating it as one among many:

It is good for us to take the initiative and to find out things for ourselves. This is an essential part of establishing oneself as a mature and self-reliant individual. But we should only do so in the context of contributing to society and other people's wellbeing all the more proficiently as a result of our self-centred activities. This can only be a short term answer that enables us to get things straight in our own minds. When we have got things clear in our heads then we compare our conclusions with others and not assume that just because we have reached clear conclusions therefore they must be correct.

Putting it into practice:

This answer is best put into practice in relation to cultural answers such as the scientific and aesthetic answers. Carrying out these answers very often means looking for answers by ourselves. Thus, we should seek our own answers in the context of the community within which such answers are being sought and discussed. To get at the truth of things we need to put our conclusions into the public arena to find out their true value. Seeking such answers for ourselves is also part of the educational process. We achieve self-improvement by exercising judgment, formulating opinions for ourselves, and thereby becoming more self-reliant.

Ancillary answers:

We are here to serve our own ends alone. This answer takes solipsism to its logical conclusion. A person who thinks only of him or herself and has no thought for others would be labelled autistic. Such a person could hardly function as a sociable being. However, to have ends to be fulfilled implies having some language skills to formulate these ends, and this would bring us into the social sphere in the course of understanding and gratifying our ends. Perhaps the most purposeful and end-driven person must also be the most sociable persons if they are to accomplish their ends with any success.

What Can We Make Of These Answers?

We can make of these answers only as much as we find within us to make anything of them. But in looking to ourselves alone we inevitably arrive at very limited answers to the questions that we pose ourselves. Even geniuses need in the end to refer back to their fellow mortals to share their would-be discoveries or innovations with other people. Even Nietzsche's Zarathrustra gets fed up of his own company and comes down from the mountains to share his prophecies. Unfortunately, as is often the case with would-be prophets and geniuses, he found precious few ears willing to listen to him.

11
Reflex Responses

- ➤ *The Aggressive Answer:* **We are here to be aggressive and forceful**
- ➤ *The Humble Answer:* **We are here to be humble and submissive**
- ➤ *The Dissembling Answer:* **We are here to be all things to all men**

What's Reflex About Them?

These answers are reflex responses because they refer to three reflex types of behaviour in which people react to situations in a stereotypical way instead of a thoughtful and flexible way. Individuals who are subject to these reflex reactions, become more notorious than respected for them. They have tendencies, genetic or environmental, which lead them to adopt these respective kinds of behaviour and become habituated in them. In so far as these answers are reflex reactions means that something can be done about them. In the absence of clear evidence to the contrary, we must assume that people can alter such reflex reactions if they have a will to do so.

The reflex nature of these ways of living does not preclude any genetic or hereditary factors in influencing or originating them. These seem only to be influences and not absolute determinants of our behaviour. That they are only influences is suggested by that fact that some people with such tendencies also show an ability to control and overcome their tendencies in one respect or the other.

The Aggressive Answer:
We are here to be aggressive and forceful

What this answer means:

This answer refers to the tendency of some people to believe that they have to be aggressive and forceful to get things done or to get their own way. It means that aggressiveness and forcefulness has become such a way of life to such people that they are considered to have aggressive and forceful personalities because they consistently behave in aggressive and forceful ways. They are not necessarily inherently or genetically inclined to be aggressive and forceful. The fact is that their aggressive behaviour has become so ingrained that they have become nothing but aggressive and forceful people. It is more a matter of bad habits than of bad genes.

A very harsh view of our aggressive tendencies is taken by the psychiatrist, Anthony Storr, in the Introduction (p.9) to his book, *Human Aggression*:

> The sombre fact is that we are the cruellest and most ruthless species that has ever walked the earth; and that, although we may recoil in horror when we read in newspaper or history book of the atrocities committed by man, we know in our hearts that each one of us harbours within himself those same savage impulses which lead to murder, to torture and to war.

Recent animal research has shown that even the great apes are not free of cruelty, aggression and even murder and genocide. We have simply become more technologically efficient in committing atrocities. Storr ought also to take account of our potential innocence of such matters. We are not prone to aggression provided we are not placed in situations that bring out our aggressive tendencies instead of sublimating them by directing them towards civilised purposes. In short, our aggression can be socialised if we train ourselves sufficient well to direct it towards productive projects.

What this answer is good for:

This answer is good for reminding us that there is a place for aggressive and forceful behaviour in human affairs. Often very little would be achieved if we behaved all the time in a non-aggressive and unforceful manner. Sometimes the situation may require that we lose our tempers, thump tables, and throw our weight around to get things done or to right some wrongs. Human beings can be aggressive and forceful when they chose to be so and it serves no useful purpose deny this fact.

What's wrong with it:

This answer is wrong in that we are not necessarily intended to be aggressive and forceful animals. The fact that we behave like that does not mean that we must at all times in the future behave in such a manner. It is wrong to think that aggressive and forceful behaviour is tolerable as a way of living since people would always be fighting one another like primitive tribalists. Aggression and forcefulness for itself own sake is the epitome of uncivilised conduct. Unfortunately the violent imposition of religious beliefs and political ideologies is still prevalent so that the peripheries of civilisation are still beset with violent tribalism at this time.

Treating it as one thing:

To be aggressive and forceful all the time is to render oneself obnoxious to other people. It is counterproductive to one's personal aims in life if one is branded as being an entirely aggressive and forceful person. Such a person is avoided by others and is brought the attention of police and security officers when behaving aggressively and forcefully in public places. Even when the aggressive and forceful person gets their own way, trust and respect from other people are replaced by fear and loathing.

Treating it as one among many:

There is a place for aggression and forcefulness as part of our repertoire of reactions to the various situations we are confronted with in life. It is a matter of learning to control our aggressive impulses and channel our forcefulness towards sociable and rational pursuits. We need a certain amount of drive and severity to get things done. Shrinking violets do not achieve much just as overly aggressive people often fail because of their behaviour and not because of the invalidity of their point of view or the inappropriateness of what they are trying to do.

Putting it into practice:

This answer is best put into practice only in those situations where no other response but aggression and forcefulness seems appropriate and necessary. The appropriate way to put this answer into practice is to develop the judgement and discrimination required to make use of aggressive and forceful feelings and channel them into those activities where they can do more good than harm. Anger management classes are one fashionable way of dealing with this problem.

Ancillary answers:

We are here to assert ourselves because might is right. This is the answer of bullies, tyrants and dictators. They think that life is driven by the exertion of power over other people. This attitude is the product of deep personal insecurity. They suffer from a fear of not being up to the mark to succeed in life, therefore they must force themselves on others willy nilly. Plato argues this attitude away in the first book of his *Republic*. As against the view that justice belongs to the strong person, he shows that it makes things worse rather than better because the strong person is not right because of their strength but because they have done the wise and reasonable thing. Strength is supposed to be used for the benefit of other people and not simply to dominate and intimidate them.

The Humble Answer:
We are here to be humble and submissive

What this answer means:

This answer means making humbleness and submissiveness a fundamental part of our personalities to the extent that we respond to everything in life with those characteristics. In response to any social contact we behave humbly and submissively as if we were not worthy of deserving of such contact. We hide behind that kind of behaviour and make it an excuse for not doing as much with our lives than we might have done otherwise. We are here to be humble and submissive in appropriate circumstances but not necessarily in all circumstances whatsoever.

What this answer is good for:

This answer is good for stressing the importance of behaving in a humble and submissive way in appropriate circumstances. Being humble and submissive on some occasions is part of being human since it means that we are recognising our limitations as human beings. It is appropriate that we should feel humble and behave submissively in the presence of someone for whom we have great respect and admiration. We admire famous people who in spite of their fame behave humbly and do not make out to be superior persons merely because they have come to public notice through their achievements.

What's wrong with it:

This answer is wrong because humble and submissive behaviour is not a good thing in itself. To make a habit of behaving humbly and submissively in all circumstances whatsoever is to make it a permanent feature of one's personality. A permanently humble and submissive person is asking to be stood on and taken advantage. It is characteristic of a person possessed of what used to be called an inferiority complex.

Treating it as one thing:

Humbleness and submissiveness are inadvisable traits when they are so ingrained that the individual is nothing but a humble and submissive person. To ingratiate oneself to everyone on every occasion is a revolting trait that makes Uriah Heap such an abominable character in Dickens's novel, *David Copperfield*. Humble and submissive behaviour can invite a violent and contemptuous response since people feel no respect for such behaviour. In fact, such behaviour can invite bullying and intimidation which might be avoided if the person learnt to stand up for themselves.

Treating it as one among many:
To behave humbly and submissively on appropriate occasions is something we all need to learn. It is a great antidote to the tendencies towards aggression and forcefulness which characterise the previous answer. But we need to be flexible and discriminate about where and when we behave humbly and submissively. Humble behaviour is the antithesis of proud and overbearing behaviour. They are extremes that are to be avoided without overlooking their value in the circumstances where they may be called for.

Putting it into practice:
This answer is being put into practice when we find ourselves in any situation which is truly humbling and makes us feel submissive. We might have such feelings not only in the presence of someone whom we admire but also in an awe-inspiring place such as in great cathedral or on top of a mountain. We are humbled by great works of art and literature and ought to be inspired to make similar outstanding contributions to human culture.

Ancillary answers:
We are here to find our place in society however lowly. This involves an abject submission to the class system probably out of insecurity. It signifies a need to lose oneself in the herd so that one no longer needs to strive to be anything in particular. Perhaps a person suffers disabilities that make them feel their lowliness and insignificance in society. But every human being is valuable in themselves, no matter how insignificant they may feel themselves to be.

The Dissembling Answer:
We are here to be all things to all men

What this answer means:
This answer means behaving as if one had no personality or inner life of one's own. For it means responding to people according to how they expect us to behave rather than how we ourselves want to behave. It is the attitude of the play actor who is used to assuming the personality of whatever character they are meant to play on stage, film or television. If the actor lacks a clear view of their own personality then they may have

difficulty knowing how to be themselves in ordinary society. For example, the actor and comedian, Peter Sellers is said to have been unsure of his own personality in that way.

Instead of behaving to people according to a consistent inner picture of who we are, the dissembling person varies their responses constantly according to how they think that they are expected to behave. They become all things because they can behave in a friendly way when they think they are expected to be friendly, a hostile way when they think they are expected to be hostile, and similarly, in a confiding way, a cheerful way, and so on. They tend to put on the appearance of being hardworking, trustworthy, honest, reliable, merely because it is expected of them and not because they themselves like to behave in such ways.

What this answer is good for:
This answer is good in that we should take account of other people's feelings in the way we behave to them. It is good for emphasising the adaptability of our behaviour. Often by behaving consistently in ways that we are expected to behave, we begin to behave habitually in that manner. In fact, it is by mimicking the behaviour of other people that we learn the correct ways to behave before we have the sense and independence of mind to work out for ourselves how to behave. The problem is that the dissembling person brings such mimicry into adulthood and fails to learn how to think and act for themselves.

What's wrong with it:
This answer is wrong in that it can be seen as an anti-social trait in which the individual is never to be relied upon or trusted to be themselves. What they really think and feel is never revealed because they don't know themselves what they think or feel. In so far as this behavioural trait is anti-social it does the individual no credit whatsoever. It leads to unprincipled conduct because the dissembling individual lacks inner standards of behaviour by which to control and limit their responses to other people. It is also wrong to adopt an attitude of always trying to be all things to all men in so far it is an attempt to be popular and likeable. One becomes popular and likeable for the way one behaves rather than for what one really is within oneself.

Treating it as one thing:
If everyone behaved in such a way as to be all things to all men then trust and honesty would be the first casualties. We rely on people saying what

they mean and behaving according to their sincere thought and feelings. A person who is all things to all men, cannot be true to others because they cannot be true to themselves. The Jesuits in their missions to far eastern countries adopted the policy of being all things to all men so that they were able to adapt their missionary techniques to the peoples in which they found themselves. This introduces a measure of insincerity and insinuation which did them no credit. It doubtless led them to be discredited in seventeenth century Japan which closed its doors to western culture as a result.

Treating it as one among many:

An ability to adapt to other people's needs and to the exigencies of any situation is useful to us all. This answer makes sense as part of a strategy of being a sociable and adaptable person. We want to make ourselves amenable to other people but not to the extent of eliminating consistency of behaviour and being totally unprincipled. Principles and good habits of conduct are built up through making use of other answers which help us to build up a inner picture of who and what we are as individuals.

Putting it into practice:

This answer is put into practice when we change our colours according to the environment in which we find ourselves. It is inevitable that we should adapt our behaviour to some extent according to the people we find ourselves with or according to changing circumstances. However, there are limits to which this can be pursued without engendering insincerity, distrust and falsehood. When we are deliberately deceiving people about our true feelings, beliefs or opinions then we are committing bad faith that does us no credit. If it is done at all, it can only be to spare other people's feelings and because it is the best course of action from a moral point of view, as for instance in the case of bereavement when a person's feelings are catered for more than one's own. If a person is dying of cancer, there is the difficult moral question of whether a doctor or relative should or should not inform the person of that fact. It may depend on whether they need to know this or not.

Ancillary answers:

We are here to be anything we care to be: This humanistic answer is often misused by confidence tricksters and charlatans who wish to exploit other people. It is used to justify lying, deceit, fraud and downright dishonesty. It is only true in so far as the world is our oyster and it is up to us to make the best of our opportunities. But it is taken to undesirable extremes when we go around defrauding people and conning them. It is only a valid answer when it is used strictly in association with the sociable and cultural answers discussed above.

What Can We Make Of These Answers?

We can make limited use of these answers in behaving as flexibly as possible in response to differing circumstances. They help us to learn when to be aggressive, when to be humble, and when to change our behaviour according to the demands of whatever situation we find ourselves in. But they require to be applied in a limited and circumscribed fashion so that they do not become behavioural traits which label us as such for a lifetime.

12
The Self-Sacrificing Responses

> ➢   *The Self-Penalising Answer:* **We are here to suffer and live in pain.**
> ➢   *The Great Cause Answer:* **We are here to sacrifice ourselves to a cause greater than ourselves**
> ➢   *The Self-Immolating Answer:* **We are here to sacrifice ourselves for the sake of others.**

What's Self-Sacrificing About Them?

Self-sacrifice means putting one's selfish concerns aside. The object towards which the sacrifice is directed is treated as more important than oneself. Our own lives, health, well-being or pleasures become secondary to other people's suffering, causes, or well-being, for which we willingly or unwillingly sacrifice ourselves. The above answers involve self-sacrifice which may or may not be laudable and justifiable. The mere fact that self-sacrifice is involved does not mean that the situation, person, thing or whatever is worth sacrificing oneself for. We often sacrifice ourselves for no good reason. Self-sacrifice which is taken too far is not commendable but plain stupid. Thus, we make fools or heroes of ourselves by our self-sacrifices and we are never quite sure whether we are being the one or the other. There is thin dividing line which makes it impossible for us to be objective about the true value of our self-sacrifice. Other people must often be relied upon to make that judgment and we just do what we have to do. The best we can do is to cultivate our own judgments regarding our own conduct, that is to say, by gaining more self-knowledge.

The Self-Penalising Answer:
We are here to suffer and live in pain

What this answer means:

This answer means that suffering and pain are regarded as an unavoidable part of life. From the time we are born we have no right to expect anything else in life but an unending succession of painful events in which we suffer grief, hardship, illness, misfortune or whatever. Whether this is the case or not is a matter worthy of debate. It is arguable that, nowadays in our comfortable consumer society, life is not necessarily full of suffering and pain. We might not inconceivably have fun and laughter from the day we are born till the day that we die, and never know what it is to suffer or be in pain. Young and healthy individuals living in a prosperous society may have little or no inkling of real suffering or pain in their lives. In fact, their lives may be so free of these drawbacks that they contrive circumstances to ensure that their lives become extremely painful and insufferable. They may take to drink, drugs, self-abuse, food disorders, fanatical or obsessive behaviour, fast cars, or dangerous sports to make their boring lives seem more interesting and challenging.

What this answer is good for:

This answer is good for telling us that life is not meant to be easy. Pain and suffering can enrich our lives because they make sure that we don't take life for granted. We appreciate the simpler things better in life when we have experienced discomfort as for instance when suffering hardship in the wilderness. It is good to suffer and good to take pains. Without either of these during some period of our lives we hardly know what life is. As animals we were built to struggle for existence, therefore it is not good for us to have too easy a life. We need hardship, trials and tribulations not only to test us but also to make us give of our best.

What's wrong with it:

This answer is wrong because suffering and pain is to be avoided and can often be avoided. Something is wrong if we are continually suffering and in pain. It is not natural even for animals and plants to suffer and feel pain excessively. They try to avoid pain and suffering as much as we do, even when they have no control over their circumstances. What other living beings undergo results more from the vagaries of fortune or misfortune. We are supposed to have achieved an ever-increasing control over our lives and the conditions under which we must live. Therefore, there is less and less reason for us to experience any more suffering and pain than is produced by our own ignorance, stupidity, and misjudgment. We often have no one to blame except ourselves for our suffering when our own behaviour or misbehaviour has brought it about. Also, believing that life is full of pain and suffering can become a self-fulfilling prophecy. We go out of our way to get the pain and suffering which we expect to have.

Treating it as one thing:

It is a very sad and distressing view of life to place such emphasis on pain and suffering that it is regarded as the principal and unavoidable part of life and living. To want pain and suffering in excess is a pathological condition to which sad, sado-masochistic people are subject. Such people require treatment much more than encouragement to indulge in their pathetic practices. The German philosopher, Schopenhauer took the view that our lives are inevitably full of suffering and pain because we are wilful creatures whose will is constantly being thwarted. According to him, when we fail to get what we want, this induces suffering. He is making more out of 'suffering' than our common sense view of the word. Nowadays, we would regard the starving peoples of underdeveloped countries to be suffering. We suffer if a relative or friend dies suddenly, is killed in a car crash or a bomb explosion. But Schopenhauer thinks that we suffer merely when our desires and goals are thwarted. We suffer simply when we don't get what we want. This seems to be the philosophy of the spoilt child or immature adult. Moreover, he contrasts suffering with boredom. According to him if we are not in pain or suffering then our lives are boring and empty. He goes even further to argue that the aim of wisdom is to deny and thwart the will. Thus, his aim is to promote and invite suffering instead of avoiding it.

Treating it as one among many:

Pain and suffering may be an unavoidable part of life but there is no reason nowadays why anyone's life should full of nothing but pain and suffering. People living centuries ago or in medieval or classical times had to put up with much more pain and suffering than most of us nowadays. The prevalence of disease, famine, violence, penury must have made many people's lives pretty unbearable. We have the power to make our own lives freer of suffering and pain than any other culture in history. But if we make too much of eliminating these then they will spring up in some other form as human beings have always had a penchant for making life difficult for themselves, even if just for the hell of it. We all need just enough pain and suffering in our lives to enable us to function effectively as human beings. We reach maturity and responsibility as adults when we have learnt to balance the extremes of easy living with the discomforts of activities that challenge our mental and physical capabilities. Thus, for example, one might live in ease and comfort in a hotel in the Alps while daily challenging oneself with rigours and privations of mountain climbing and off-piste skiing.

Putting it into practice:

This answer should not be rationally and deliberately put into practice as if it were the one and only answer in life. It is senseless for us to create any more pain and suffering for ourselves when it is already part of our lives. We cannot make sense of this answer unless we have already experienced suffering and pain. Putting it into practice can only mean that the individual expects to find pain and suffering to be a significant or dominant part of their lives. However, the expectation can be a self-fulfilling prophecy. Those who expect to suffer pain and misfortune in their lives may find their expectation fulfilled because that expectation leads them to seek it out. It should be put into practice only in relation to the solipsistic answers which involve enjoying and pleasing ourselves.

Ancillary answers:

We are here to get very fat or very thin: There are no limits to the extremes that people will go to in making themselves suffer needlessly. They may eat too much or starve themselves too much. What begins as a pleasurable or laudable pursuit is all too often taken to extremes where it causes more pain and suffering than anything else. Yet people can persist unto death in their obsessions. One can only hope that increasing self-knowledge and inner development can fortify people against become enslaved with such self-harming obsessions.

The Great Cause Answer:
We are here to sacrifice ourselves to a cause greater than ourselves

What this answer means:

A 'cause' in this context is an ideal or objective which is taken up by an individual or group of individuals who regard the ideal or objective as important in itself. They will consider it to be so important that they are prepared to sacrifice themselves in specific ways to achieve it. The ultimate sacrifice is of course to die for the cause which they regard as being great because of the benefits accruing from achieving the objectives of the cause. In certain states of mind, we envy those people who have a cause to which they dedicate their lives without reservation or self-doubt. But the righteousness of those dedicated persons is not justified simply by the fact that they are willing to sacrifice themselves to such a cause. The true and lasting value of the cause is the only valid criterion by which the cause is to be judged, and certainly not the fervour of its adherents. It is also debatable whether we should be envious of those who need to sacrifice themselves so single-mindedly. The need to do so perhaps signifies an inner privation or failing which cries out for compensation.

What this answer is good for:

This answer is good for drawing attention to causes and the good and the harm they can do us. Causes are good for making us put up with pains and inconveniences about which we would otherwise complain or get angry. It is good to emphasise the importance of sacrifice as something that human beings enjoy doing. Sacrificing yourself for a cause can make you feel better. The fact that you believe the cause to be greater than yourself makes you feel that you are adding value to your life because of that sacrifice.

The uplifting nature of Great Causes:

The best causes are uplifting and inspiring, but so much human faith and energy has gone into causes which have brought out the worst in human nature. For example, people were thrilled and inspired by the great cause of Nazism in pre-war Germany, and turned a blind eye to its faults. The good feelings that it gave people were symbolised in the evocative scene in the feature film, *Cabaret*, when the young boy stands up in crowded outdoor cafe and begins singing 'Tomorrow belongs to me'. A splendid and inspiring song, one feels. But slowly the camera pans out to reveal that this impressive youngster is a member of Hitler Youth. It has no political content but it was used as a Nazi recruiting song and those who join him in singing are uniformed Nazis. It is to our everlasting shame that such noble feelings can be inspired by the very worst of causes; in this case, the twisted ideas of a misanthropic megalomaniac who based them on the most inhuman and retrograde aspects of the Germanic tradition. Our ever-abiding task is to ensure that our feelings are inspired only by the best and most laudable of causes. This difficult task is eased by having a healthy scepticism about the value of any putative 'great cause'. This applies as much to long-standing causes as to those which are entirely new since they all have great potential for harm when treated as great and consuming causes.

What's wrong with it:

It is wrong to make too much of sacrificing ourselves for anything in this life because it is doubtful whether anything is of such intrinsic or extrinsic value to justify such sacrifice. We may be demeaning and lowering ourselves in thinking that a particular cause is great enough to warrant our sacrificing time and effort in support of it. The greatness of any cause is only in the mind and it is difficult to prove beyond any doubt that a cause is really great enough to warrant the sacrifice that we are making on behalf of it. A cause is no more than a belief which is treated as if it were an all-encompassing truth. It can be blown out of all proportion to its actual importance in human affairs as a whole.

Treating it as one thing:

When the great cause becomes greater than our lives or the lives of others then the value of the cause becomes questionable. The great cause of sacrificing ourselves for God, King and Country became more and more questionable during the course of the twentieth century. It became increasingly unfashionable to beat these drums, and the decline of the British Empire was the inevitable result of making too much of that cause.

People who consider themselves to be great of heart and spirit are particularly vulnerable to the lure of the great cause. They have immense feelings and abilities within themselves that they wish to give out and share with others. This may be termed the 'Sir Galahad' complex, after the knight who dedicated his life to finding the Holy Grail. But it is really an emptiness inside themselves that they are trying to fill by reaching out to whatever comes to hand. They need to look to other things in life to bring the nature of the feelings into perspective.

Treating it as one among many:

Sacrificing ourselves for a greater cause than ourselves can be a part of our lives without becoming the be-all and end-all of life. Most people are doing this nowadays when they support their families, when they look after others more assiduously than they look after themselves. They also sacrifice themselves in working for an organisation with whose aims they are totally in sympathy. They are genuflecting to the greater cause of helping that organisation. But they can do so without sacrificing other aspects of their lives – their family, friends, hobbies and interests. The attitude of the professional person is that their sacrifice is limited to the workplace and that they value a well-rounded lifestyle in conjunction with their work.

Sacrifice is good because it can make us feel better but to ensure that the cause really warrants our sacrifice we must look to other answers to help us. What are needed are adequate criteria for judging the true worth of any cause. Such criteria can only be found by looking outside the circumstances governing that cause. This means taking into account other answers to the problem of living.

Putting it into practice:

We put this answer into practice when we make a great deal of something to the extent of seeing no limits to the extent to which the cause is to be implemented or sacrificed for. This alone must put us on our guard and make us treat the great cause with enough scepticism to see it in its true perspective. This answer is best into practice by reference to solipsistic and other answers which might serve to moderate the fervour of devotion to a cause. We should have more going on in our lives than just the one great cause. For we need to turn our attention away from a dominant interest to keep it in perspective.

Ancillary answers:

We are here to submit to the will of great men and sacrifice ourselves for them: This answer reflects a propensity of human beings to make gods out of mere men. Even the ideal of liberal democracy to make us all equal and get rid of class distinctions and personality cults cannot erase this propensity. Hence the adulation of 'superstars' in music, sport and other fields. The whole celebrity culture reflects this unfortunate irrationality. Needless to say, the worship of Hitler led to millions sacrificing themselves in this manner, and to no lasting purpose.

The Self-Immolating Answer:
We are here to sacrifice ourselves for the sake of others

What this answer means:

This answer differs from the one above in that the cause is focused on the welfare, well-being or improved future of other people. Sacrificing ourselves for others means putting aside our own lives, safety, desires, goals, views, opinions or whatever so that others may benefit from our actions or lack of action. It means that we care for others more than we care for ourselves. The sacrifice therefore involves some inconvenience and privation to ourselves. It is not a sacrifice if it makes no difference to us whether we do something for others or not. It is no sacrifice to give money to the poor when one has plenty of it. You might feel better about yourself by giving things to other people but this is not a sacrifice unless it hurts and inconveniences you in obvious ways. Sacrificing ourselves for others is not only laudable but also one of the most appealing of human traits. However, like every other human activity it can be taken to harmful extremes, for instance, when we make mindless slaves of ourselves for the sake of others.

What this answer is good for:

This answer is good for making us value the lives of others and show that we do in fact value their lives. We are demonstrating what we feel about other people in our heart of hearts. When we put such an answer into practice we reveal the extent to which we are thinking of the welfare of others. It is good for us to put the well-being of others before that of ourselves. We feel better about ourselves and we add meaning and significance to our own lives as well as to the lives of others. We should do this all the time as parents, lovers, friends, associates or whatever. It is only human to feel for other people and to want to do things for them. Our humanity is never more in evidence than when we willingly make sacrifices for others.

What's wrong with it:

It is wrong to think that any person is really worth sacrificing ourselves for to the extent of harming or diminishing ourselves in any degree. No human being is so much more important than any other human being that the latter should make inordinate sacrifices for the sake of the former. This answer is deficient because we might be putting too much value and significance on the person for whom we are sacrificing ourselves. It is wrong to make so much of sacrificing ourselves that we become slaves to the needs and desires of other people. We become slaves when our own needs, desires, aims, hopes and aspirations are sacrificed entirely and those of other people take their place entirely. We allow ourselves to be a mere cipher or a worse than useless thing in comparison to the object of our enslavement. In other words, we cease to be a viable and self-respecting human being. This kind of slavery is not worthy of any human being as it decreases our humanity rather than enhances it. It is a worse state of mind even than that of sacrificing ourselves entirely for a great cause.

Treating it as one thing:

If we spend our lives doing nothing but living for others and caring nothing for ourselves then the chances are that we are underrating ourselves and our abilities and talents. We are making life easy for ourselves at one level to escape the responsibilities of individual freedom. We are not only allowing other people to do our thinking for us, we are also living our lives through them. We have no life to call our own. However commendable self-sacrifice might be, it needs to be kept in proportion like every other human activity. Taken to extremes, it means submitting oneself to the will of others. Humanity involves sacrifice for the sake of others but inhumanity results from complete slavery to the whims and desires of others. What we do for other people makes us human in so far as it is done within a limited context. When the context is undefined and unlimited then the demands of others erode our humanity and diminish our self-esteem to make us worthless in our own eyes.

Treating it as one among many:
It is an essential part of all our lives than we make sacrifices for others. Otherwise we are nothing but heartless loners who live only for themselves. But it is equally essential part of our lives that we think of ourselves and our own interests. Parents often feel the need to sacrifice themselves in some way for the sake of their children's well being and future. They can do so without feeling that their sole purpose on Earth is to do nothing but sacrifice themselves for the sake of their children. Such self-sacrifice for their children's sake is as harmful to the children as to the parents. For the children are not only spoilt but may also fail to learn to put limits on their demands on the world.

Putting it into practice:
We put this answer into practice whenever we put other's welfare before that of our own. The problem is that our feelings can take over and prevent us from making balanced judgments as to whether we are going too far in our sacrificing ourselves. Again the solipsistic answers in particular serve to mitigate the excesses of sacrificing ourselves for others since we must also think of ourselves to make sure that we do not exceed the bounds of common sense in our sacrifices. Learning to use common sense, in this context, is a matter of maturity of attitude and achieving a level of balanced thought.

Ancillary answers:
We are here to dedicate ourselves to the good of others: This is a more religious answer and also less self-sacrificial than the above. It has perhaps more in common with the 'humanist answer' and with the *Sociable Responses* such as the '*Co-operative Answer*'. Dedication is an important part of our altruistic tendencies.

What Can We Make Of These Answers?
These answers are very comforting because they provide simple and straightforward ways of coping with the problem of living. It is easy to fall into them and allow them to take possession of our lives. However, such easiness means that they are easily taken to extremes. In so far as they are

intimate to ourselves as individuals, they are potentially damaging to us. They can motivate us into worthwhile and productive lives when they are applied within strict limitations. Therefore, we should make as little as possible of these answers. They are false idols which delude and mislead us.   Therefore, these answers are useful guides to the problem of living because privation and self-sacrifice can bring a great deal of meaning and significance to our lives.

Conclusion

How to use these answers

All the answers discussed above are interrelated in that they refer to or involve other answers. Indeed, some answers might relevant to all of the others. For instance, the hedonist answer relates to every other answer in so far as we seek pleasure in whatever we are doing. We should aim to get at least some enjoyment at some stage. Also, an answer such as 'we are here to be nice to each other' reminds us that we can benefit personally by being nice to everyone we meet on a daily basis. Similarly, in taking account of every other answer, we can pack as much as possible into every aspect of our lives. We should do so simply because it is in our own interests to do so if we are make the most of our lives.

It has been argued continuously in this book that the monistic way is to be avoided. To take one of these answers as being the only answer and to disregard all the others is potentially to cripple the personality and reduce the capacity to make the most of life. Ideally, we should keep all these answers before our mind as we go through life. We ought always to entertain the possibility of changing our approach to life by giving more emphasis to one or more of these answers over the others. However, we inevitably slip into ruts and rigid habits of thoughts, and this possibility is all too easily forgotten.

Believing in the possibilities facing the human race is a matter of attitude and not of truth, knowledge or experience. We must adopt that viewpoint as a matter of personal policy to benefit from it personally. Nothing that anyone can know, reason about, or experience, is sufficient in itself to convince them that it is necessary to have faith in future possibilities. Only a change of mind or *metanoia* can accomplish this. You either see it or you don't. Perhaps this book will help individuals to achieve this crucial change of mind, without which the future of the human race must forever remain in doubt. A clear majority of us need to believe in humanity's future so that we can all do what is necessary in practice to make a better future for ourselves.

But how can we know that a universal change of mind of this kind would be desirable and would achieve the aim of giving direction to human affairs? And how can we be sure that it will not lead to brainwashing, indoctrination, and other authoritarian and inhuman practices? This change of mind would be desirable if it gives people more security concerning their own futures and their own place in society. Humanists don't need authoritarian methods of persuasion, since they are continually trying to convince themselves of the worthiness of their own arguments. They wish to take account of every person's arguments against their own, without suppressing them in any way. They must not only continue to develop their arguments to the point of convincing others, but also show the benefits of such beliefs by the good works they lead to and by the example they set in living by them. Thus, a change of mind may be achieved by combining the force of reason with good works and good example. Anyone who remains unconvinced, even by these best efforts, is probably unable or unwilling to think in universal terms and therefore must be left alone with his solitary, solipsistic thoughts. 'Live and let live' is a key policy in humanism.

Making the most of our freedom to choose

This book may help people to make the most of their freedom to choose. They need to be clear about what they want out of life, otherwise a surfeit of choices combined with an inability to choose between them may lead to a **fear of freedom**, to use the title of a notable book by Erich Fromm.[*] Not being clear about our choices may be because of an insufficiently developed personality. We lack a developed and integrated system of thought by which choose clearly between alternatives. We are unable to formulate coherent aims and goals by which choices may be made. As a result, there is apprehension, instead of elation, at the range of choices and opportunities which life has to offer. Unless we have in mind certain aims and goals to help us to cope with these choices and opportunities, we may recoil from freedom altogether and eagerly accept the nearest chains and restrictions which will provide a feeling of security, however temporary or illusory. Thus, we narrow our range of choices, and submits to the authority of an external palliative, such as one of those listed above; anything that will make life seem bearable, even if it only serves to stave off lasting solutions to the problems that pursuing one's aims and goals give rise to.

[*] Cf. Erich Fromm, *Fear of Freedom*, (1942 - London: RKP, 1960) pp. 93, 106 etc.

To make the most of our choices it is necessary to participate actively in human society. And the bigger the unit of human society, the greater are the range of choices at our disposal. Thus, our range of choices reaches a maximum when it is equal to what is available to the whole human race. In this view, freedom comes from recognising that one forms part of a larger pattern to which one can contribute, however modestly, by doing as much as possible with one's life for the best possible reasons.

A useful distinction can be made between the pursuit of individuality and the personalisation of the individual. To pursue individuality for its own sake is to strive for absolute freedom as an end in itself. To personalise ourselves on the other hand is to aim for universal values which are beyond us in belonging to the language culture in which we are born. These values are not new or startling; they are the ethical values such as good, bad, just, unjust. They help us to articulate our aims and goals in terms of the rational alternatives available in the society we belong to. We become persons in our own right through these rational, social ties, rather than isolated individuals who are alienated and have no sense of belonging or contributing to society.

This distinction is important because the mere pursuit of individuality disintegrates society into competing units, while personalisation integrates society in terms of common interests. The former leads to a polarising plurality, which gives civilisation no future, while the latter points to a future in which a *convergence* of personalities takes place as they organise themselves in terms of aims and goals that are common to them all. All this is not so much a conclusion as a start to working out systematically how to integrate all the choices listed in this book in terms of our personal needs and aspirations. Thus, the importance of the unity of humanity is argued for in greater detail in my books *Belief Beyond Belief: Looking to a Better Future* (Almostic Publications, 2017), and *Advancing Humanity: The Need to Make Our Own Future* (Almostic Publications, 2016).

Printed in Great Britain
by Amazon

14433624R00081